GLORIANA

GLORIANA

ELIZABETH I & THE ART OF QUEENSHIP

SIOBHAN CLARKE & LINDA COLLINS

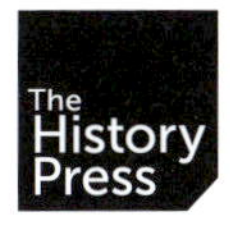

First published 2022

The History Press
97 St George's Place, Cheltenham,
Gloucestershire, GL50 3QB
www.thehistorypress.co.uk

British Library Cataloguing in Publication Data.
A catalogue record for this book is available from the British Library.

ISBN 978 0 7509 9754 6

Typesetting and origination by The History Press
Printed and bound in Great Britain by TJ Books Limited, Padstow, Cornwall

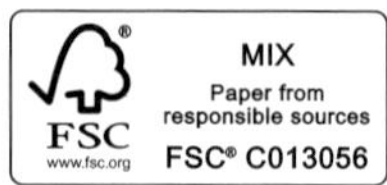

Trees for LYfe

CONTENTS

LIST OF ILLUSTRATIONS

8   *The Hampden Portrait* by Steven van der Meulen (or George Gower), *c.* 1563, oil on canvas transferred to panel. Private collection. © CPA Media Pte Ltd/Alamy

9   *The Sieve Portrait of Elizabeth I* by Quentin Metsys II, *c.* 1583, oil on canvas. Pinacoteca Nazionale, Siena. © Keith Corrigan/Alamy

10   *Portrait of Queen Elizabeth I* by Nicholas Hilliard, 1595–1600, watercolour on vellum (miniature). Royal Collection Trust / © Her Majesty Queen Elizabeth II 2021

11   *The Phoenix Portrait* by Nicholas Hilliard, *c.* 1573/75, oil on panel. Tate Britain, on view at National Portrait Gallery, London. © Incamerastock/Alamy

12   *The Pelican Portrait* by Nicholas Hilliard, *c.* 1573/75, oil on panel. Walker Art Gallery, Liverpool. © IanDagnall Computing/Alamy

13   *The Rainbow Portrait* by Isaac Oliver (?), *c.* 1600, oil on canvas. Hatfield House, Hertfordshire. © IanDagnall Computing/Alamy

14   *Portrait of Sir Francis Walsingham*, attributed to John de Critz the Elder, *c.* 1589, oil on panel. © National Portrait Gallery, London

15   *Portrait of Mary, Queen of Scots in Captivity*, after Nicholas Hilliard, inscribed 1578, oil on panel. © National Portrait Gallery, London

16   *Portrait of William Shakespeare (Chandos Portrait)*, attributed to John Taylor, 1600/10, oil on canvas. National Portrait Gallery, London. © Bridgeman Images

17   *Portrait of Philip Sidney* by an unknown artist, *c.* 1576, oil on panel. National Portrait Gallery, London.© Prisma Archivo/Alamy

INTRODUCTION

GLORIANA

Writers have portrayed the life and reign of Queen Elizabeth I for centuries – in books, plays and films – and the fascination remains today. Easily one of our most popular monarchs, in 2002 she was among the list of '10 Greatest Britons' in a BBC poll. She is admired as a successful leader and a woman ahead of her time who is an integral part of England's national story. But her early life was full of uncertainties and she was an unlikely candidate to be the greatest offspring of Henry VIII. This daughter, by Anne Boleyn, was the wrong sex in a world governed by men and she was often considered illegitimate because her parents' marriage was annulled. The odds were stacked against her, but Elizabeth would survive the vicissitudes of her siblings' reigns, numerous Catholic plots to kill her, the formidable Spanish Armada and the most obvious obstacle of all: her gender.

On becoming Queen, Elizabeth needed a very strong image to unite her country and consolidate her power. Art was a powerful device for displaying royal magnificence and for propaganda but a mere likeness would never be sufficient. Elizabeth's portraits increasingly relied on glittering jewels, gowns and accessories for the projection of majesty. Along with her formidable grasp of public relations, her persona was a vital ingredient of her rule. The 'Cult of Gloriana' developed towards the end of her reign, a movement in which authors, musicians and artists – such as Spenser, Shakespeare, Tallis, Byrd and Hilliard – revered her as a virgin goddess, unlike other women. It was an idea sustained by public spectacle, chivalry, sonnets and oration which paid homage to Elizabeth as a deity. The Queen's image was widely owned and distributed for the masses, thanks to the expansion of printing and, for the wealthy, through the medium of the painted portrait.

Elizabeth's England was a small kingdom on the fringes of Europe which grew in self-confidence, in no small part because of the Queen herself. Her long reign provided domestic peace and stability, allowing the arts to flourish so that the Elizabethan era would prove to be a 'Golden Age'. The eighteenth-century antiquarian Horace Walpole said in his *Anecdotes of Painting in England* that there 'was no evidence that she had much taste for painting, but she loved pictures of herself'. Successive periods in history have invested her reign with significance and a large part of this legacy is her captivating image.

ELIZABETH I AND THE THREE GODDESSES

Hans Eworth, 1569, oil on panel, Royal Collection Trust

The allegory referred to in this painting is the Judgement of Paris, a theme derived from Greek mythology which also became popular in Roman art. Three of the most beautiful goddesses, Venus, Juno and Minerva, compete for the prize of a golden apple, dedicated 'to the fairest'. Jupiter, King of the Gods, was intended to judge the competition, but instead he nominated Paris, Prince of Troy, to carry out the task. Paris chose Venus as the winner on the strength of her promise to help him win the hand of the most beautiful woman alive, Helen, the wife of Menelaus, King of Sparta. (It was Paris's seduction of Helen and his refusal to return her that led to the Trojan Wars.)

The panel can be visually divided into two sections. To the left-hand side, Elizabeth is emerging as though onto a stage. She enters the scene through a classical archway leading from a substantial brick building. Inside the open door of the structure can be glimpsed a gold coffered ceiling, a frieze containing the Tudor coat of arms and a canopy displaying her own arms. She is wearing a crown and carrying an orb and sceptre, the most powerful attributes of monarchy. Her ladies-in-waiting are deep in conversation and are perhaps unable to see the vision before them. They are superfluous to the allegory, but they serve to ground the Queen in reality. Elizabeth would not have travelled anywhere without her accompanying ladies.

The right side of the picture is allegorical, with the three goddesses presenting a riot of movement and vivid colour. They are set into a pastoral landscape that includes a depiction of Windsor Castle and Venus's chariot drawn by swans.

As the painting was commissioned either by Elizabeth or as a gift to her, the Queen would have been expected to take centre place in the composition. However, she has been supplanted by Juno, the goddess of marriage and fertility. Juno, Queen of the Gods, is gesturing for Elizabeth to follow. The position of her arm is echoed by the curved neck of the crowned peacock, her sacred bird. But Elizabeth will not be enticed by Juno's association with matrimony and family life.

In the middle of the three allegorical figures is Minerva, the goddess of battle strategy and wisdom, whose powers include bestowing heroes with courage. She wears a helmet and a breastplate embellished with the head of a gorgon, and she carries a standard. The gorgon, with its hair of venomous snakes, was given to Minerva by Perseus as protection. Anyone looking at a gorgon was turned immediately to stone. In common with Elizabeth, Minerva, the warrior maiden, was believed to remain perpetually a virgin.

On the far right is Venus, the goddess of love, beauty, pleasure and passion. Her discarded smock belongs to the age of Elizabeth rather than a world of myth. Its distinctive and colourful embroidery is typical of Tudor design of this time. The broken arrows on the ground, the bow and the discarded quiver refer to Venus's son Cupid, who tried in vain to shoot Elizabeth with his darts of love. The implication is that despite her beauty, Elizabeth is impervious to matters of the heart.

The goddesses reflect the choices Elizabeth has made to rule wisely. Juno represents Elizabeth's rejection of marriage and children, Minerva emphasises her skill, wisdom and courage in battle and Venus alludes to the Queen's

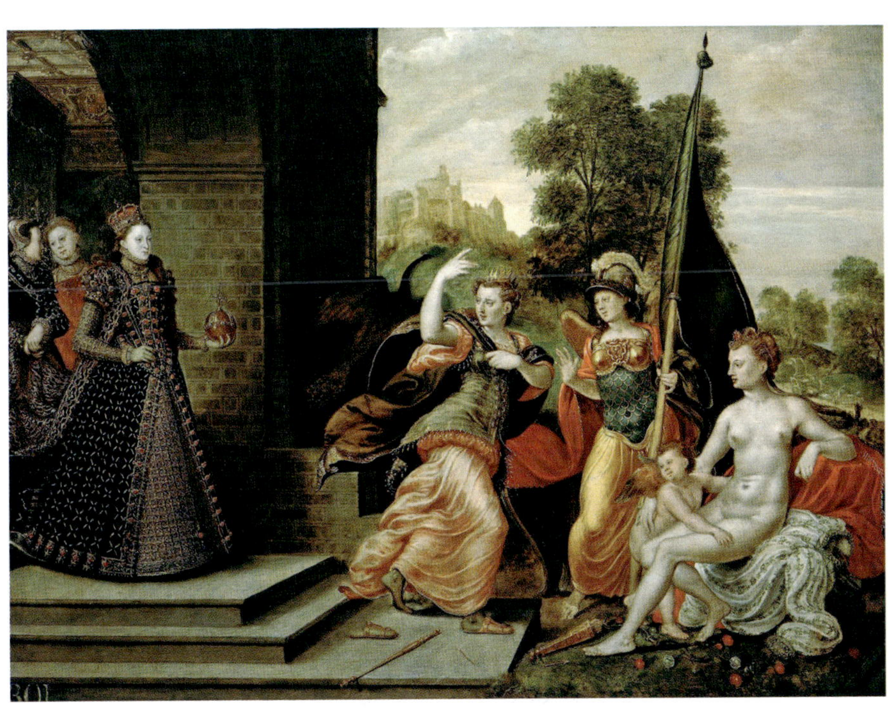

Elizabeth I and the Three Goddesses is intended to reflect the Queen's rejection of marriage and children, her courage in battle, her wisdom and her beauty.

beauty and the life of pleasure that she has rejected, enabling her to govern her nation wisely. And yet, it is Elizabeth who retains the prize – not a golden apple but a golden orb, a powerful symbol of monarchy that represents the Queen's triumph over all three of these classical goddesses.

The first record of this picture is in 1600, in a diary written by Baron Waldstein, a German nobleman, who had seen it at Whitehall Palace. It was sold for £2 in the Commonwealth sale in 1652 to 'Hunt and Bass', of whom little else is known, but it returned to the Royal Collection during the reign of James II. On the frame is written: 'Pallas [another name for Minerva] was keen of brain, Juno was queen of might, / The rosy face of Venus was in beauty shining bright, / Elizabeth then came, And, overwhelmed, Queen Juno took flight: / Pallas was silenced: Venus blushed for shame.'

The identity of the artist has been disputed. The initials 'HE', painted on a rock in the lower right corner, are suggestive of the artist Hans Eworth, although art historian Roy Strong considers the initials were originally 'HF' (Hoefnagel *fecit*) referring to the Flemish painter Joris Hoefnagel, noted for his topographical views and his mythological subjects. The landscape and the painting of Windsor Castle bear similarities to the Hoefnagel picture *The Marriage Feast at Bermondsey*. At present, the Royal Collection has attributed the painting to Hans Eworth, the artist from Antwerp who is associated with complex allegorical works and with the design of sets and costumes for Elizabeth's court entertainments.

There are two points of interest unrelated to the meaning of the picture – it is believed to present the earliest pictorial representation of Windsor Castle and it is the only known portrait of Elizabeth wearing gloves. It is the first known allegorical portrait of Elizabeth and, to appreciate the image, viewers needed to interpret the classical messages contained in the painting. Elizabeth is depicted moving forwards from a dark interior into the light of the 'new learning' and the Renaissance.

I

ELIZABETH I AND THE ENGLISH RENAISSANCE

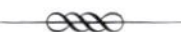

Elizabeth acceded to the throne of England in 1558 following the death of her half-sister Mary I, and inherited an England that had been divided by bloody religious turmoil. The nation had also suffered defeat in a French war, which had lost Calais and shaken confidence.

Under Elizabeth's rule, the religious turbulence of the previous reigns grew calmer as the Queen avoided the religious extremism of her siblings and the Protestant Reformation became less contested. England's centralised government was well organised and efficient. A third of the population still suffered in poverty but for the most part there was an atmosphere of peace and growing prosperity. Overseas ventures opened new trade routes that had a positive effect on the Elizabethan economy. Painting, poetry, theatre, literature and music flourished, supported – as all arts need to be – by the economic growth of the country.

Throughout Elizabeth's reign, painting continued to be dominated by portraiture, as it had been during the rule of the preceding Tudor monarchs. However, Elizabethan portraiture lies in the period between the death of Holbein (in 1543) and the arrival of Van Dyck (in 1632); it rarely gives us an insight into the true personality of a sitter in the frank manner of the former or the dignified style of the latter. Full of signs and symbols, the chivalric, courtly interpretations by Elizabethan artists often hide from us the face of the living person. Foreign artists, principally those originating from the Netherlands, still monopolised artistic production in England due to their superior painting skills. However, in the genre of miniature painting, English artists began to find distinction not only at home, but also abroad. Elizabeth's court artist, Nicholas Hilliard, forged an international reputation and was the first English artist to find fame in Europe.

There was no established art market through which artists could sell their works and so, to sustain themselves and their families, they depended on the patronage of prosperous supporters. For reasons of wealth and prestige, the Queen and her courtiers were highly sought-after patrons.

After her father, Henry VIII, Elizabeth is the most familiar to us of the Tudor monarchs, because during her reign the collecting and display of portraits became increasingly popular. It was possible to buy a ready-made portrait of the Queen to display in private homes, universities, guildhalls and town halls. Full-length portraits became popular due to the novelty of a whole person standing in front of you.

The most potent influence on all the arts in England was Elizabeth herself. The young Queen was initially presented as the embodiment of sexual virtue, to defend her from charges of unfitness to rule due to her sex. As she aged and it became clear that she would leave no heir, so the Queen became vulnerable and her realm potentially unstable. Youthful and flattering face patterns of Elizabeth had been employed by artists from around 1575. Soon after 1590 (when the Queen was in her sixties), the artist Nicholas Hilliard invented a smoother-skinned and more exaggeratedly youthful image of her known as a 'mask of youth'. This did not just improve on the Queen's image as the face patterns had done, but replaced her true features. From then onwards, she was rarely painted as elderly but as an ageless beauty who represented the eternal nature of monarchy and the magnificence of the nation. Patterns of this mask were distributed to artists to copy, ensuring that the Queen's public image was always consistent and ever youthful. Submitted to the judgement of her Serjeant Painter, George Gower, any portraits of the Queen produced after around 1596 that did not conform were destroyed. The subterfuge of this 'Cult of Gloriana' lasted almost until the Queen's death in 1603 when she was approaching 70.

To reinforce her timeless image, the Queen's clothes for portrait sittings required careful consideration and Elizabeth's women of the Privy Chamber looked after their care. The most notable among these ladies was Blanche Parry, who also managed the Queen's jewels. An inventory of 1587, compiled by Blanche on her retirement, revealed that Elizabeth had 628 pieces of personal jewellery. Blanche was twenty-five years older than the Queen and had served her for fifty-seven years, forsaking marriage and children to devote herself entirely to her mistress. Her family were from Herefordshire and in

2015 a piece of embroidered fabric was discovered in the Parry family church of St Faith in the small Herefordshire village of Bacton. It had been kept as an altar cloth, but it is believed to have originally come from a dress worn by Elizabeth I. Out of more than 1,900 spectacular dresses that the Queen owned at her death, this is believed to be the only surviving fragment. It was probably given as a gift to Blanche and it appears to have originated from the elaborate gown Elizabeth wore in the *Rainbow Portrait*. This is the most puzzling painting of Elizabeth ever completed and one that will be discussed in Chapter Six.

The art of embroidery was an important skill for Elizabethan women, children and sometimes men. Church vestments, altar hangings and chasubles (outer vestments worn by a priest when celebrating mass) had been decorated with needlework since medieval times but embroidery was increasingly used for secular purposes during the Tudor period. There was a developing taste for rich, colourful embroidered domestic furnishings and clothing. Almost all young girls were taught how to sew, a talent that was viewed as a mark of their diligence and piety. Elizabethan 'samplers' (pieces of material on which the various stitches were practised) can occasionally still be discovered in auctions and antique markets, usually embellished with the date and name of the needleworker. For those of the lower socio-economic classes, sewing and making clothes was a practical skill that could provide an income. For the daughters of the nobility, the ability to produce elaborate and decorative embroidery was an accomplishment that would complement their roles as mistresses of large households.

Elizabeth admired and supported all the arts and she enjoyed both popular entertainment and the higher arts. She attended events such as bear baiting and cock fights as enthusiastically as music recitals or classical plays and poetry readings. Her understanding of poetry and literature was widened by her ability to speak, read and converse in six languages.

The Queen enjoyed music and was an accomplished player of the lute and the virginals. As well as composing music and singing, she danced with grace and expected her courtiers to be able to do the same. New types of musical instruments led to changes in musical composition. An early violin was invented, along with a form of oboe that produced a more complex arrangement of sounds, meaning that Elizabethan music became more expressive and emotional. Sacred music (particularly that with Latin lyrics) evoked Catholicism and during Elizabeth's Protestant reign it became less frequently performed. And yet the Queen enjoyed church music and appointed Thomas Tallis, who had formerly composed for Mary I, to her Chapel Royal. Tallis had been present at Elizabeth's coronation and was considered one of England's greatest composers, best remembered for his choral music. It is an example of Elizabeth's religious tolerance that he was joined in the Chapel Royal by William Byrd, another Catholic composer. A form of secular music known as the madrigal was invented in Italy, but by the mid-sixteenth century it had largely fallen out of favour in Europe. In Elizabethan England, however, the madrigal was increasingly acclaimed. Byrd popularised the English form of madrigal, a love poem for four to six voices, which he set to music with English lyrics.

All creative artists aspired to the patronage of the Queen or her courtiers and, in many instances, she inspired their plays, poems and music. In his poem 'The Shepheards Garland, III', published in 1593, the poet Michael Drayton styles Elizabeth as Beta, 'the Queene of Muses'.

Perhaps the most ambitious poem written during the reign of Elizabeth I was Edmund Spenser's *Faerie Queene*, first published in 1590. It is one of the longest poems in the English language, although it was never completed; his original plan was to write twelve volumes, with each one focussing on a different moral virtue. The books contain two principal characters, a 'Prince Arthur', who represents the legendary King Arthur of medieval romance, and the 'Faerie Queene Gloriana', symbolising Elizabeth. It is set in a mythical land where the Queen is offered 'mirrours more than one' in which she can see herself reflected. In the same work, she is associated with Belphoebe, a virgin huntress personifying the goddess Diana, a reference to Elizabeth's chastity. Belphoebe falls in love with Timias, so Spenser is encouraging the Queen to fall similarly in love, renounce her virginity and produce an heir. The writer hoped to gain royal favour through his work and the Queen responded by awarding him a lifetime pension of £50 per annum. For comparison, a statute given at Westminster in 1588 lists an employed brewer as earning £10 per annum and a butcher £6. The Masters employing them would have earned a greater salary but Spenser's pension still appears very generous. It would have afforded him a comfortable lifestyle even without his other commissions.

Thomas Wyatt had introduced the sonnet into England in the early sixteenth century. It originated in thirteenth-century Italy, when Petrarch had perfected it to write about his love for a married woman named Laura. A sonnet is a lyrical poem that is traditionally fourteen lines long. The first eight lines outline the predicament and the following six lines resolve it. Its form was changed in English to comprise three quatrains (a series of four lines) and a two-line rhyming couplet. Sir Philip Sidney, an Elizabethan poet, courtier and soldier, popularised the English sonnet to express unrequited love. He penned 108, but none were published before his early death in battle at the age of 31. In English, these emotive and imaginative pieces were often set to music in the form of a madrigal.

Much of Elizabethan poetry has faded from popular consciousness, but the work of William Shakespeare continues to be widely read and performed to avidly interested audiences, a testament to a writer who composed some of the greatest literature of all time. Shakespeare's first narrative poem, *Venus and Adonis*, is an erotic work of more than 1,000 lines, based on a myth from the Roman poet Ovid's *Metamorphoses*. Shakespeare turned it into a comic poem in which a goddess tries unsuccessfully to seduce an uninterested young man. It was written in 1592 as plague closed the London theatres, denying Shakespeare his usual means of income. In 1594, he published *The Rape of Lucrece*, taken again from the work of Ovid. These poems were extremely popular and were reprinted many times. Shakespeare continued writing and produced a sequence of 154 sonnets that gained him a reputation as a serious poet and a chronicler of the Elizabethan age.

At the time, authors were restricted in what they could write and how they could express themselves, so plays for the theatre tended to be written in allegory, where they presented contemporary problems and criticised political situations in a disguised form. Prior to 1598, the majority of playhouse plays were written anonymously or with the name of the author disguised for fear of finding themselves in prison or worse. Ben Jonson was arrested and imprisoned for *The Isle of Dogs*, a play he co-wrote with Thomas Nashe in 1597, although it was suppressed so completely that no copy exists to explain his crime today.

Throughout the arts, it was abundantly clear to writers that they were expected to glorify the Queen.

In the field of decorative arts, the demand for silver grew quickly during the reign of Elizabeth. There had been a rapid rise in population and the expanding middle and upper classes sought quality domestic silver to furnish their new and impressive homes. In 1564, the Company of Mines Royal was established to 'search, dig, roast and melt all manner of ores of gold, silver, copper and quicksilver in the counties of York, Lancaster, Cumberland, Westmoreland, Cornwall, Devon, Gloucester, Worcester and Wales'. The directors of the company included Elizabeth's chief advisor, William Cecil, Lord Burghley, her favourite Robert Dudley, Earl of Leicester, and William Herbert, Earl of Pembroke, politician and courtier. Elizabethan silver is often lavishly decorated with fruit, vegetation and grotesque figures, reflecting the European taste for Renaissance design, but, as the century wore on, decoration became less elaborate. Silver goods were fashioned in London to match the highest European standards and around the country centres, such as Norwich in Norfolk or Exeter in Devon, were producing top-quality pieces of plate. Unlike artists, who did not generally sign their work, silversmiths tended to mark their plate designs with their initials or various marks, including a fish, a sun or a cross.

In 1572, Elizabeth gave away gifts of silver weighing almost 6,000 ounces. It was a popular commodity with a growing market. The wooden and pewter spoons of Henry VIII's era were now supplanted by those made of silver. As the Elizabethan age progressed, it became fashionable for more varied items to be produced in silver, such as sconces, mirrors, lustres and jars. As these secular items were being fabricated, so ecclesiastical silver was being melted down. Today, few ecclesiastical pieces made prior to the reign of Elizabeth survive.

The Queen's goldsmith from around 1558 to 1576 was the unusually named Affabel Partridge, a London-based craftsman whose trademark was his exceptional quality and lavish embellishment. When Elizabeth came to the throne in 1558, she commissioned a new Great Seal, the device employed by the Chancery to show that the attached document had been approved by the Queen. When a monarch died, their Great Seal was destroyed. Elizabeth's half-sister Mary's seal had been intentionally damaged after her death to render it obsolete and Elizabeth gave it to her new Lord Keeper of the Great Seal, Sir Nicholas Bacon. In the 1570s, Bacon commissioned Partridge to melt down Mary's seal and use it to make three gilt silver cups, one for each of his three houses in Hertfordshire, Suffolk and Norfolk. Partridge engraved Bacon's coat of arms on the bowl of the cups, along with a boar – a pun on the name Bacon. The Norfolk cup is in the collection of the Ashmolean Museum in Oxford, acquired with support of the Art Fund in July 2021 from the collection of Sir Ernest Cassel, a British merchant banker. A second cup has resided in the British Museum since being bequeathed in 1915. The whereabouts of the third cup is unknown. Hallmarked in London, they are among the few surviving pieces by Partridge, connected to the Elizabethan court and demonstrating the immense skill of the Queen's goldsmith.

Elizabethan architecture became a distinctive feature of the English countryside as wealthy courtiers built themselves lavish prodigy houses. In summer, Elizabeth would travel the country on progresses to visit and lodge at these elaborate abodes. As she was accompanied by as many as 500 attendants in her retinue, her stay represented an enormous expense for the host. It was considered a great honour to be selected for a visit by this parsimonious monarch, who built no great houses or palaces herself.

Builders of the time modified the quadrangular medieval layout, omitting one side, resulting in an 'E'-shaped building that permitted sunlight and air to circulate more freely. The Great Hall on the ground floor was generally where the most expensive art and sculpture was situated and where guests were invited to be impressed. It was now used less than in the time of Henry VIII, with the Long Gallery running above the Hall becoming the centre of Elizabethan entertaining and family living. It was still uncommon, in England, for houses to be designed by architects; usually the owner worked in collaboration with builders and stonemasons. One of the first architects in England was Sir John Thynne, steward to Edward Seymour, 1st Duke of Somerset, who in 1549 was already designing a great house at Longleat. Thynne employed the master mason and architect Robert Smythson, a designer of manor houses who went on to design Hardwick Hall in Derbyshire and Burghley House in Lincolnshire.

Encouraged by new advances in science, England looked abroad and Elizabethan seafarers explored uncharted areas of the globe. Martin Frobisher landed on Baffin Island, Humphrey Gilbert in Newfoundland and Walter Raleigh was awarded a charter to colonise Virginia. Controversially, Elizabeth backed privateers, such as Francis Drake and John Hawkins, who raided Spanish and Portuguese ships, bringing the gold back to fill English coffers. Henry VIII had founded the Royal Navy but, of his three children, it was Elizabeth who prioritised its strength. It seems fitting, therefore, that during her reign 'Britannia', a Minerva-like female warrior, wearing a helmet and holding a trident and shield, should be employed as the female personification of England.

The reign of Elizabeth I was an era of great expansion in all fields of the arts. It was a time of world exploration and of achievements that inspired national pride and embodied a feeling of great optimism. It was also an age of conspiracies and plots against the Queen as she faced continual threats to her life and reign, both religious and political. Her Secretary of State, Sir Francis Walsingham, built up an ongoing network of spies and used his contacts to gather intelligence information from across Europe to ensure the Queen's safety.

Elizabeth died in 1603 after a reign of almost forty-five years. The sun finally set on Gloriana, as the last Tudor monarch died in her own bedchamber, having taken reluctantly to her bed. As Sir Walter Raleigh said, 'she was a lady surprised by time'.

2

FAMILY AND SURVIVAL:
THE EARLY YEARS

The child who would become 'Gloriana' was born at Greenwich Palace on 7 September 1533, the daughter of Henry VIII and his charismatic second wife, Anne Boleyn. She was named Elizabeth after both her grandmothers, and her gender was a bitter disappointment. Planned celebrations for Henry's long-awaited son were cancelled and the letters prepared to announce the birth of the 'Prince' were hastily changed by the addition of a scribbled letter 's'. The King had broken from the Church of Rome to marry Anne and secure his dynasty with a male heir, who was expected to become a great king in years to come. In an age when the hand of God was seen in everything, this birth was a terrible reversal of fortune. Nobody would have predicted that Henry's true heir had indeed been born that day in Greenwich and that Anne Boleyn's daughter would one day reign over an English 'Golden Age'.

FAMILY

Before Elizabeth reached 3 years old her mother was executed on charges of adultery with five men, and her father, Henry VIII, signed the death warrant. In spite of this, she grew up admiring her father, while also acknowledging the mother she could not remember. As Queen, she would adopt Anne's falcon badge and she wore a mother-of-pearl locket ring, set with gold and rubies, which bore both her own and her mother's portrait inside.

From babyhood, Elizabeth was established in her own household and lived at several royal properties north of London. The most well-known is the red brick fifteenth-century palace of Hatfield and it was here that her nursery years began. Her sister Mary, who was seventeen years older, lived at Hatfield until after the fall of Anne Boleyn and then had separate establishments at Beaulieu (also called Newhall), Richmond and Hunsdon.

The tiny princess, now known as 'the Lady Elizabeth', was entrusted to the care of Margaret Bryan, her Lady Governess, who thought her 'as toward a child … as ever I knew any in my life' (meaning that the infant was remarkably advanced for her age). There was some lack of funds in the household, following Anne's fall, as Elizabeth began to outgrow the rich clothes lavished upon her by her mother. Lady Bryan reported to Secretary Cromwell that she 'has neither gown nor kirtle nor petticoat nor linen for smock'. The following year, Margaret Bryan was transferred to the service of a more important infant:

the baby Prince Edward, who arrived in October 1537. Elizabeth had lost her first foster mother but her care was taken over by two surrogate mothers who would be part of her life for decades. Blanche Parry was Elizabeth's former cradle-rocker and Kat Ashley joined the household as her governess. Both would love and protect the girl through her formative years and beyond.

The children of Henry VIII lived mostly in separate establishments but records show that both sisters were attentive to their little brother, visiting when they could and bestowing gifts. Edward looked like Elizabeth, they were close in age and they shared a love of books but, according to Lady Bryan, he 'took special content' in Mary's company. It's possible that his mind was more like Mary's. They both held a fanatical belief in their one preferred form of Christian worship, which they would try to impose on their country, while Elizabeth occupied the middle ground.

The rise of humanism had helped the cause of education for upper-class females and Henry VIII wanted all his children to have the learning of a good Christian prince. Elizabeth was a natural academic and, like her brother, she benefited from the teaching of distinguished tutors. The best known is the Cambridge scholar Roger Ascham. He said, 'Her mind has no womanly weakness … her perseverance is equal to that of a man, and her memory long keeps what it quickly picks up.' The princess received schooling in history, philosophy and the tenets of her father's new Church of England – a subject that would ultimately shape her country. She also had a fascination and aptitude for languages. She was well tutored and excelled in both Greek and Latin, the two major languages of learning and philosophy. In addition, she became fluent in French, Spanish and Italian, attainments of which she was very proud. In years to come, on formal visits to Oxford or Cambridge, Elizabeth spoke casually in Latin and she used Erasmus's Latin version of Petrarch as a source text for her translation of the Italian poet's poems. Her earliest surviving letter is written in Italian, in 1544, to Henry's sixth wife, Katherine Parr. At New Year, when it was traditional to exchange presents, the 11-year-old Elizabeth sent Katherine her own translation of the French devotional work *The Mirror of the Sinful Soul*, with an embroidered cover, worked by her own hand. Similarly, in 1545 she presented Henry VIII with an embroidered prayer book containing a copy of Katherine Parr's *Prayers or Meditations*. In her own flourishing script, the child had translated it into Latin, French and Italian. It is conserved today in the British Library in London, where it remains the only surviving letter from Elizabeth to her father.

Queen Katherine was an affectionate stepmother who did much to reconcile the King with his daughters. It's also possible that by the time of his last marriage the ageing King had given up hope of fathering another son. In July 1543 Parliament passed the third Act of Succession of Henry VIII's reign, which restored both Mary and Elizabeth to the throne, behind their half-brother. On the slight shoulders of Edward rested Henry's hopes for the Tudor dynasty but, in the unthinkable event that the boy should die, Henry's daughters could now also inherit the crown. Perhaps it was due to Henry's overwhelming authority that this contradiction between his daughters' bastardy and their standing as his heirs was never challenged in his lifetime.

An anonymous painting, entitled *The Family of Henry VIII*, marks Henry's dynastic vision. It was probably commissioned in 1545 and shows Henry with Edward and the boy's deceased mother, Jane Seymour, occupying a central space, traditionally reserved for the Holy Family. His two daughters are relegated to the outer sections of the painting and are dressed alike in French hoods and lavish damask gowns with long trains. They look almost identical in both face and dress but their jewellery is different: Mary wears a cross while Elizabeth has a necklace forming the initial 'A'. It is almost certain that Elizabeth inherited this jewel from her mother, Anne Boleyn, who owned an 'A' as well as the famous 'B' necklace. There is a theory that Henry would have disapproved of the necklace and that it was added to the painting in Elizabeth's own reign. (The picture is recorded as hanging in the presence chamber at Whitehall Palace when Elizabeth was Queen.)

We can see Elizabeth again, aged 13, in an accomplished work by Guillaume Scrots, which can be viewed in the Royal Collection at Windsor Castle. She stands in a sumptuous gown of crimson damask, a book clasped in her elegant white hands, intimating that her reading has been interrupted for the painting to be created.

ELIZABETH I AS A PRINCESS

Attributed to: Guillaume Scrots, c. 1546, oil on panel, Royal Collection Trust

This is the earliest known individual portrait of Elizabeth, painted when she was a teenager. It is unusual because it was probably intended as a private image and, by contrast, Henry VIII employed art to glorify his reputation with his court and public.

The young princess looks apprehensively at the viewer with a sideways glance. The long and slightly hooked nose, which will remain the dominant feature in all future portraits, is strongly evident, along with her distinctive gold-red hair and almost imperceptible eyelashes and brows. Her colouring, nose and mouth favour her father, Henry VIII, while her dark eyes are the legacy of her mother.

She is wearing a vivid crimson silk gown that the artist has flecked with yellow to indicate costly gold thread. The rich fabric was most likely woven in Italy and purchased from Italian merchants, such as Antonio Corsi or Lorenzo Bonvisi, who traded directly with the Great Wardrobe. The undersleeves and forepart of the petticoat are made from cloth of silver, patterned with loops of metal thread. It was a Florentine speciality known as tissued fabric and it was far more expensive than the crimson silk of her gown. Sumptuary laws restricted the wearing of tissued fabric to the royal family and so Elizabeth's apparel asserts her royal blood. For Mary and Elizabeth, portraits like this date from periods when they were in favour with their father. This meant that they would have money for clothes and would also have received items ordered on the King's warrants. Their stepmothers further provided them with gifts of clothing.

Elizabeth's finger is placed inside the book she is holding, where a piece of paper or perhaps white ribbon is used to mark a page. There is a larger tome on the table to her right which may be the Old Testament, although to date there has been no satisfactory explanation for the blank pages. The volume in her hand is perhaps the New Testament, but it could also be a religious text in Greek or Latin that was intended to hint at her learning. The Venetian ambassador, Giovanni Michiel, said of Elizabeth, 'She is a young woman whose mind is considered no less excellent than her person.'

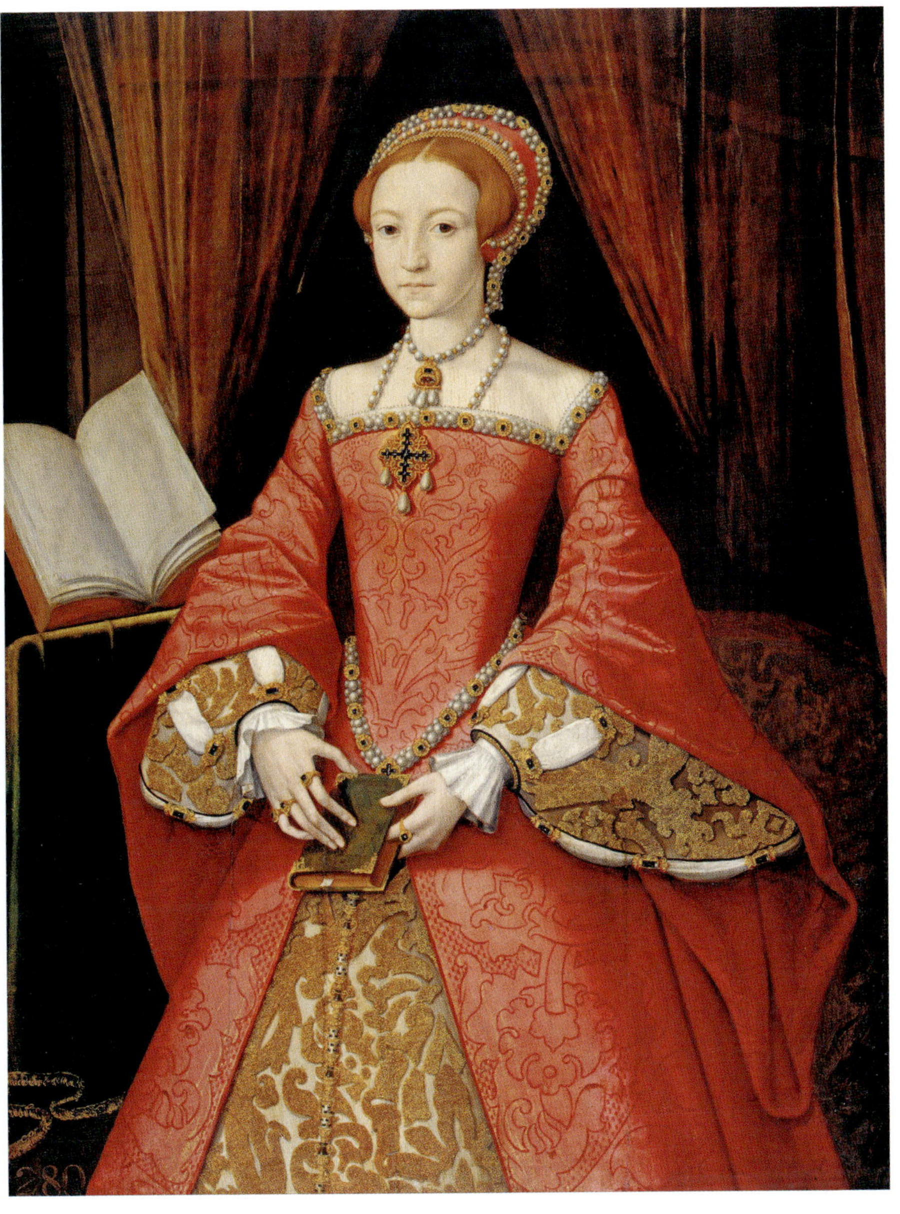

The earliest known individual portrait of Elizabeth, painted *c.* 1546 when she was a young teenager and probably intended as a private image.

Elizabeth's pride in her education is likely the theme of this painting. Originally, the portrait referenced the classics; the wall behind the large open book was composed of elegant architectural features that continued behind Elizabeth's left shoulder. The decoration contained carved rams' heads, an important motif in Roman ritual and religion, and there was a recess to the right, perhaps intended to contain a statue. Close inspection of Elizabeth's girdle (belt) is rewarded by the meticulously painted classical vases that make up its length and flow down from the book she is holding. Early changes to the picture were made before the painting was completed and the architectural details were overpainted with wood panelling and a curtain. Some of the original details are today visible through the thinning paint. During the latter part of Henry VIII's reign, artists in England continued to be viewed as craftsmen and so it was generally the patron who dictated the iconographical details – or signs and symbols – that were to appear within a portrait. Frustratingly, due to a lack of contemporary documentation, there is no explanation as to why, or on whose orders, the alterations were carried out.

The princess's jewellery is striking and beautifully painted, with pearls predominating. For the rest of her life, pearls remained the decoration of choice for Elizabeth because they represented purity and wisdom. Their round shape and white lustre associated pearls with the moon and the virgin goddess Cynthia, to whom Elizabeth was allegorically compared. It is hard to imagine from the standpoint of today, with faux pearls available at modest prices, that all the pearls painted in portraits of Elizabeth I are genuine, most likely from the Americas, and of enormous value. As Queen, Elizabeth was able to source and display huge numbers of pearls as a sign of high status because, unlike today, few of her subjects could afford to do so.

Elizabeth enjoyed wearing rings on her fingers to accentuate the beauty of her hands. Her fingers are exaggeratedly long and slim to emphasise her royal lineage, and porcelain white to confirm her high status and gentility. This is a hand that does no manual work. Elizabeth's pride in the slender beauty of her hands was to last a lifetime. In 1557, the Venetian ambassador described Elizabeth as having 'above all, a beautiful hand of which she makes a display'. The artist has slightly changed the position of her right hand and altered the position of the book she is holding, perhaps to depict it more elegantly. As with the architectural alterations, the paint has become more transparent with time, allowing the artist's modifications to become visible.

This portrait seems likely to have been intended as one of a pair, along with a painting of Prince Edward, also painted in 1546. Dendrochronology (dating growth rings in the wooden panel to the place and year they were formed) has proved that the wooden panels of the two portraits came from the same oak. They are almost identical in size and both panels were used soon after the tree was felled, with only a short time allowed for seasoning. Similar painted features appear in both portraits: for example, the tissued cloth of Elizabeth's petticoat appears in the curtains in the portrait of Prince Edward.

Both paintings have been attributed to the Flemish artist Guillaume Scrots. In 1537, he was appointed painter to Mary of Hungary, Regent of the Netherlands, and in 1545, he became painter to Henry VIII. Hans Holbein had died only two years before and yet Scrots was paid £62 10s pa, more than twice the salary Holbein had received. He remained at the English court during the reign of Edward VI but, after the young King's death in 1553, he disappears from the records, probably leaving England to return to his native Belgium.

If attributing the portraits as a pair to the same artist is acceptably conclusive, the identity of a patron has not been established and remains open to conjecture. The paintings could have been commissioned by Henry VIII, as they are listed in Edward VI's collection following his father's death in January 1547. It is also possible that Edward VI asked his sister for a portrait of herself, or Elizabeth could have commissioned it as a gift to her brother. A letter exists from Elizabeth, sent from Hatfield House, to accompany such a gesture. It is dated 12 May but, tantalisingly, there is no mention of a year nor description of content that could link it definitively to this picture. The letter reveals an interesting awareness by the princess of artistic philosophical debate. Elizabeth makes the distinction between a picture of her face, which she 'might wel blusche to offer', and that of her mind, which she will 'never be ashamed to present'. Renaissance artists and patrons heavily debated whether an artist was ever capable of capturing the mind of the sitter as well as their physical appearance and Elizabeth appears to be aware of this. She continues in her letter to her brother, separating the 'outwarde shadow of the body' from the 'inwarde mind'.

In 1546, when this likeness was painted, Elizabeth was unsure what lay ahead. Her legitimacy had been denied in the past and she would no doubt have struggled with deep insecurities concerning her future. As a young princess in this picture, Elizabeth had no idea that her brother Edward would die as a young king, nor that her sister Mary would rule for just five years, or that in only twelve years she would be crowned Queen of England. For all its secrets yet to be discovered, this portrait perfectly depicts the apprehension of a young girl facing uncertainty.

SURVIVAL

Queen Katherine continued her care of Elizabeth after the death of Henry VIII in 1547, taking the teenage girl to live with her and her new husband, Thomas Seymour (brother of Jane). However, this arrangement would soon threaten the reputation of the princess, for Seymour was handsome and he flattered her with his attentions. Elizabeth's new stepfather paid morning visits to her bedchamber, before she was dressed, where a great deal of playfulness seems to have occurred, involving romping and tickling. The flirtation went beyond what was seemly and ended only after Katherine Parr discovered the pair in an embrace and sent Elizabeth away.

Thomas Seymour's interest in Elizabeth was powerfully renewed after the death of the Dowager Queen in childbirth, in September 1548, and he hoped to marry her. His suit was rejected by Edward VI's Privy Council and the ambitious Seymour was later arrested for treason after plotting to overthrow his brother, the Lord Protector. At this point details of his former dalliance with Elizabeth emerged and she now found herself embroiled in a scandal, with rumours that she was pregnant by Seymour. It was so serious that two of her servants, Kat Ashley and Thomas Parry, were arrested and questioned in the Tower of London. The Council sent Sir Robert Tyrwhitt to Hatfield to examine Elizabeth but she answered with such confidence that he reported, 'She hath a very good wit and nothing is gotten of her but by great policy.'

At just 16, Elizabeth had survived her first crisis. It taught her a valuable lesson but may also have affected her for the rest of her life. She would never allow her heart to rule her head again. Now feeling vulnerable to slurs on her virtue, she began to dress in a sombre fashion and to guard her reputation. Perhaps she reflected on her previous flirtatious behaviour and the salacious charges levelled against her mother back in 1536. The swaggering, reckless Thomas Seymour went to the block in March 1549 and Elizabeth wrote, 'This day died a man with much wit and very little judgment.' Five years later, she would come close to execution herself as one of the most famous prisoners of the Tower of London.

The Protestant boy king, Edward VI, died of tuberculosis in 1553, having commanded (against the wishes of his father) that Mary and Elizabeth be excluded from the succession. He considered both his sisters to be illegitimate, and Mary was a Catholic. Having just approved religious reform that went far beyond the Henrician changes, he was determined to prevent a Counter-Reformation. In a will, written by his own hand, Edward left the crown to his cousin Jane Grey. Nonetheless, in a courageous gamble, the Lady Mary, now aged 37, raised her standard and gathered overwhelming support. She was proclaimed Queen in London on 19 July 1553 and, accompanied by Elizabeth, entered the city soon after to widespread joy. Mary was the first woman to successfully claim the throne of England and, if she had not fought for her right to rule, her sister might also have been excluded for ever. The question of whether a woman could wear the crown in England was settled, at last.

However, the mutual support of the sisters did not last long, due to their religious differences and tension over Elizabeth's position as her sister's heir. When

Mary ordered that everyone attend Catholic Mass, the Protestant Elizabeth had to reluctantly conform. The Queen's popularity diminished the following year when she announced plans to marry Philip of Spain.

It was taken for granted that a female sovereign needed a husband and that he should be of very high status. Philip was a Catholic prince and Spain was a long-time ally of England, so the match made good sense to Mary. But the English people feared being put under the dominion of Spain, just as a wife was naturally under the control of her husband. Marrying an Englishman would have been equally difficult because of the jealousy and resentment it would cause. Either way, a husband caused political problems for a sixteenth-century female monarch, as Mary Queen of Scots, was also to discover. Elizabeth would learn much from the marital disasters of her sister and her cousin.

Seditious pamphlets inflamed hatred against Spaniards and Parliament even petitioned Queen Mary against the union, but she was determined to go ahead. In January 1554 a serious rebellion broke out that was named after its main leader, Thomas Wyatt the Younger. The aim of the uprising was to prevent the Spanish marriage but the Queen's overthrow was also implied and her sister, as next in line, was implicated. Many had looked to Elizabeth as a focus for their opposition to Mary's Catholicism. It was a perilous position to be in.

Elizabeth was first questioned at Whitehall Palace, then told she would be removed by boat to the Tower of London. Now, in abject fear, she sat down and wrote one of the most famous letters of her life, in a desperate attempt to reach her sister, pleading, 'Remember your last promise and my last demand that I be not condemned without answer and due proof.'

The document, which is held today in the National Archives, runs on to the top of a second page. Fearing that her enemies might add false text at the end of her letter, Elizabeth struck lines through the blank space and placed her signature at the end. It is known as the 'Tide Letter'. She wrote it very slowly so that the low tide that enabled boats to pass under the arches of London Bridge had turned, sparing her from the Tower for an extra day.

On 17 March 1554 the Lady Elizabeth entered the Tower of London as a prisoner, but she did not enter through Traitors' Gate. She walked over a drawbridge at the Byward Tower as her mother, Anne, had done eighteen years earlier. It was customary for the royal family to use this private entrance and legend has it that Elizabeth fell to her knees, afraid to enter the fortress, saying, 'Oh Lord, I never thought to have come in here as a prisoner, and I pray you all bear me witness that I come in as no traitor but as true a woman to the Queen's Majesty.'

Elizabeth was held in the royal apartments (now demolished) and, although she was kept in comfort, the strain was intolerable and she often felt convinced she would die. At the same time, Robert Dudley was held in the Beauchamp Tower with his brothers, condemned for their part in the short-lived Jane Grey regime. There is a romantic story that the two young people were permitted to meet on one of the Tower walkways but there is no historical evidence to support the tale. However, it seems likely that in years to come the shared experience of imprisonment formed a bond between them.

Elizabeth was afraid but defended herself calmly under every interrogation. Her enemies, including the Chancellor, Stephen Gardiner, urged Mary to put her on trial and Simon Renard, ambassador of Charles V, Holy Roman Emperor, told the Queen her throne would never be safe while Elizabeth lived. However, Wyatt refused to implicate Elizabeth in his rebellion, despite being tortured, and he asserted her innocence in his speech on the scaffold. Eventually she was moved into house arrest and the day chosen for her release from the Tower was 19 May: the anniversary of Anne Boleyn's execution.

Elizabeth's physical and emotional survival, in the adult world of danger and intrigue, is a testament to her natural intelligence, but it may be due in no small part to the devotion of her attendants, particularly Kate Ashley and Blanche Parry, who would prove lifelong friends. They gave uncritical and whole-hearted affection to a precocious and sensitive girl, taking the place of the exalted, dysfunctional family she had lost. Later, as Queen, Elizabeth would favour her Boleyn relations and give them places at court. She chose her ladies from among her mother's relations – the Knollys, Howard and Carey families – but she was never close to her cousins of the Tudor bloodline. There is an important panel, from the middle of her reign, which makes a powerful statement about how she saw her immediate family.

THE FAMILY OF HENRY VIII: AN ALLEGORY OF THE TUDOR SUCCESSION

Attributed to Lucas de Heere, c. 1572, oil on panel, Sudeley Castle, Gloucestershire

This painting celebrates the harmony Elizabeth believed she established as Queen. In contrast to Henry's dynastic painting of 1545, which saw his daughter relegated to the wings, here is Elizabeth as his true heir. Mixing portraiture and allegory, it anachronistically shows Henry VIII, his three children and Queen Mary's husband, Philip of Spain, alongside figures from mythology. Henry, founder of the Church of England, sits on his throne in the centre, with the Protestant Edward VI kneeling beside him receiving the sword of justice. Henry died in 1547, but on the left of the picture his daughter Mary is shown next to Philip, whom she didn't marry until 1554 when she was queen, with Mars, god of war, behind them, symbolising the battles they fought in France. Elizabeth, by contrast, stands on the right of the picture holding the hand of Peace, who treads the sword of discord underfoot, as Plenty attends with her cornucopia. Henry shows, by the turn of his head, that Elizabeth will carry on the Protestant faith in England; her legitimate descent is stressed, along with her role as a bringer of peace and prosperity to the realm. Mary and Philip are both painted in darker colours, while Elizabeth, Henry and Edward are brighter, showing that they stood in the light of truth, and Elizabeth's reign is contrasted with Mary's in the same way.

Each figure is depicted wearing old-fashioned clothing that would have been appropriate to his or her reign, for example, Henry in the 1530s and Mary in the 1550s. They are also based on the works of other artists, such as the German-born Hans Holbein, and Antonis Mor from the Netherlands. All the figures are either mythical or deceased, apart from Elizabeth and King Philip of Spain, shown here wearing black Spanish dress. Philip inherited his father's Spanish Empire in 1556 and, after Mary's death, his reign in England ended.

The inscription shows that the work was a gift for Elizabeth's ambassador and spymaster, Francis Walsingham, to whose family its provenance can be traced. It was commissioned around 1572 when Elizabeth, aged 39, was beginning to see herself as the culmination

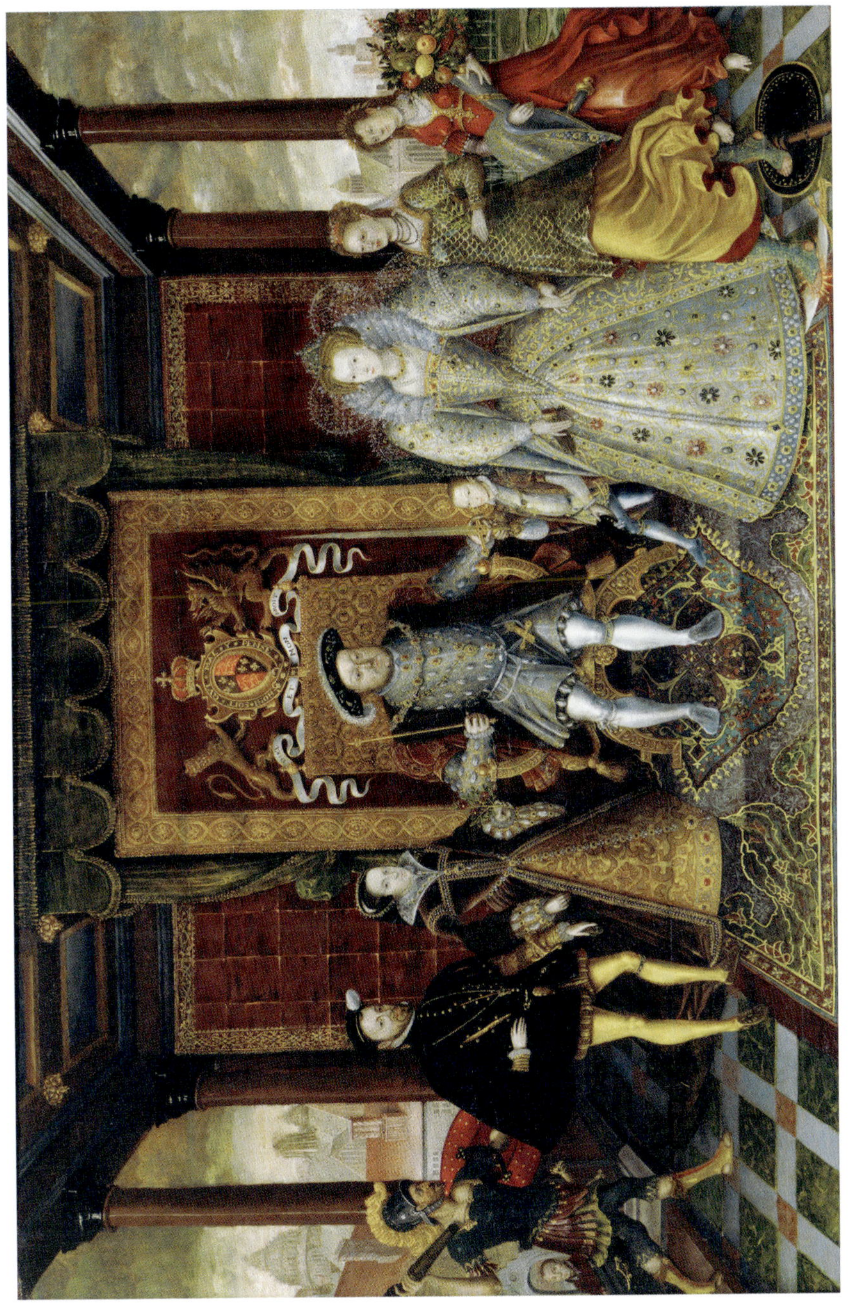

Mixing portraiture and allegory, this painting shows Henry VIII, his children and Philip of Spain. It celebrates the harmony Elizabeth believed she established as Queen.

of the Tudor dynasty. This was also the year of the St Bartholomew's Day massacre of Protestants, a shocking event in Paris which Walsingham witnessed. The picture may have been a gift to remind him of the rightness of the Protestant cause.

Lucas de Heere came to London from Ghent in the 1560s, one of many Flemish Protestant artists and crafts-people to flee religious persecution. This attribution is based upon comparison with his signed *Solomon and the Queen of Sheba* of 1559 and other works that mingle allegorical and historical personages. De Heere's fascination with costume has left an accurate glimpse into Tudor culture. The panel was purchased by former Sudeley Castle owner John Coucher Dent at the sale of the collection of Horace Walpole at Strawberry Hill in 1842 and, after being on loan to the National Museum of Wales since 1991, it has now been returned to Sudeley Castle.

⸎

Four years later, with an influenza epidemic raging, the short reign of Mary Tudor was drawing to an end and the Queen lay dying at St James's Palace. Mary had been ill from at least May 1558, possibly from ovarian cysts or uterine cancer, and Elizabeth was next in the line of succession. She was prepared to fight for her throne, if the need arose, but she didn't have to. By early November, a special envoy, the Count de Feria, arrived from Philip of Spain to tell the Privy Council how much his King desired the succession of Elizabeth. (The nearest Catholic claimant to the throne, Mary Queen of Scots, had recently married the Dauphin of France, and Philip could not permit the union of France, Scotland and England.)

Feria visited Elizabeth in the country but when he suggested that she would owe her throne to his master, she replied defiantly that the people had placed her where she was. He wrote, 'She is very attached to the people … and very confident that they take her part … She is a woman of much vanity and acumen.'

Although still only 25 years old, Elizabeth – highly educated and schooled in adversity – was more than ready for the crown and her role in history.

3

'God Hath Raised Me High': Accession and Religion

Accession

In the early morning of 17 November 1558, Queen Mary I died and for generations afterwards the date would be celebrated as Elizabeth's 'Accession Day'. At Smithfield in the City of London, Protestant heretics were saved, moments before the fires were lit, after a royal messenger announced the Queen's death. Mary's cousin, Reginald Pole, the last Catholic Archbishop of Canterbury, passed away later the same day, of influenza, and the Counter-Reformation in England died with him.

The Lords of the Council rode to Hatfield where, according to legend, they found Princess Elizabeth reading a book under an old oak tree in the grounds. The dangers of past years now turned to deliverance as they presented her with Mary's ring. Elizabeth sank to her knees and said, '*A domino factum est istud, et est mirabile in oculis nostris*' ('This is the Lord's doing; it is marvellous in our eyes': Psalm 118:23).

It is very likely that Elizabeth had prepared her speech in advance, knowing that her sister was dying. Now, she embraced her power but she also realised from the outset that good counsel was essential. Within hours she appointed two trusted servants who would become the mainstay of her regime: Sir Thomas Parry and Sir William Cecil. Parry had been Elizabeth's financial manager and now became Controller of the Queen's Household. William Cecil was a grammar-school boy who had studied a humanist curriculum at St John's College, Cambridge. He already had experience of high office, as principal secretary to Edward VI. The shrewd and industrious Cecil reassumed this role for Elizabeth and for the next forty years would be at her side as her chief minister. She called him her 'Spirit'.

Elizabeth made a triumphal entry into the City of London a week after her accession and she was crowned quickly, within two months, to invest her as soon as possible with the full authority that anointing conferred. The proceedings of a coronation fell into four parts: possession of the Tower of London; the sovereign's progress through the city to Westminster; the ceremony itself in Westminster Abbey; and, finally, a celebratory banquet in Westminster Hall.

The day before her coronation, Elizabeth set out in magnificent procession from the Tower to the Palace of Westminster. Many who watched in the snowy London streets may have also witnessed her mother's coronation twenty-five years earlier. Along the way, triumphal arches expressed themes of political and religious allegory. The first arch, at Gracechurch Street, near today's Leadenhall Market, featured large effigies of Henry VII, Elizabeth of York, Henry VIII and Anne Boleyn, with Elizabeth seated in majesty at the very top. It pointedly underlined her dynasty and the legitimacy of her succession.

On Sunday 15 January 1559 – a date that astrologer Master John Dee had determined would bring good luck – Elizabeth entered Westminster Abbey in her coronation robes, patterned with Tudor roses and trimmed with ermine. Here she was crowned by Owen Oglethorpe, Bishop of Carlisle. After the ceremony, the Queen left the abbey, smiling and exchanging greetings with the crowd. The next stage was the procession to Westminster Hall for the banquet where she came forth in a 'rich mantle and surcoat of purple velvet'. (Sumptuary laws decreed that the colour purple was only associated with the immediate royal family.)

Elizabeth's coronation was the last occasion on which the Latin service was followed and she was crowned with full Catholic ritual. However, the new Queen had made no promise to maintain her sister's faith and, in fact, a reversal was expected. Certainly, in London the pageants and speeches of her coronation demonstrated that the people of this city – who had witnessed so many Protestant burnings – now saw Elizabeth as their saviour.

QUEEN ELIZABETH I (CORONATION PORTRAIT)

Unknown English artist, c. 1600, oil on panel, National Portrait Gallery, London

Although it is considered a portrait, there is remarkably little of Elizabeth I on view in this panel painting. The picture is principally a depiction of the gold and silver coronation robes, elaborate jewellery, high ruff, ermine fur and symbolic coronation regalia. The viewer is probably not intended to see it as a portrait, but as a representation of Elizabeth's position as Queen of England. In other words, we are being shown the body politic rather than the body mortal. Under medieval and Tudor political theology, the body mortal is subject to all the infirmities of nature and will age and die as all humans do, but the body politic represents the ongoing role of government that will continue long after the monarch's death.

The gold-edged ruff rises magnificently to Elizabeth's ears so that only her face is visible. She is depicted as beautiful by sixteenth-century standards. Her hairline and eyebrows are plucked as it was believed that a high hairline made the face look slimmer and longer. Her flowing golden-red hair is loose and in the style of a young virgin, which was traditional for the coronation of a queen. When Elizabeth's mother, Anne Boleyn, was crowned consort in 1533, it was noted that her hair was long enough for her to sit on. The only other visible parts of Elizabeth's body in this portrait are her hands, which are white and bedecked with gold rings set with precious stones.

But it is the spectacular gold coronation robes that dominate the painting. First worn by Elizabeth's half-sister Mary for her coronation in 1553, they were placed in store until Elizabeth's coronation at Westminster Abbey

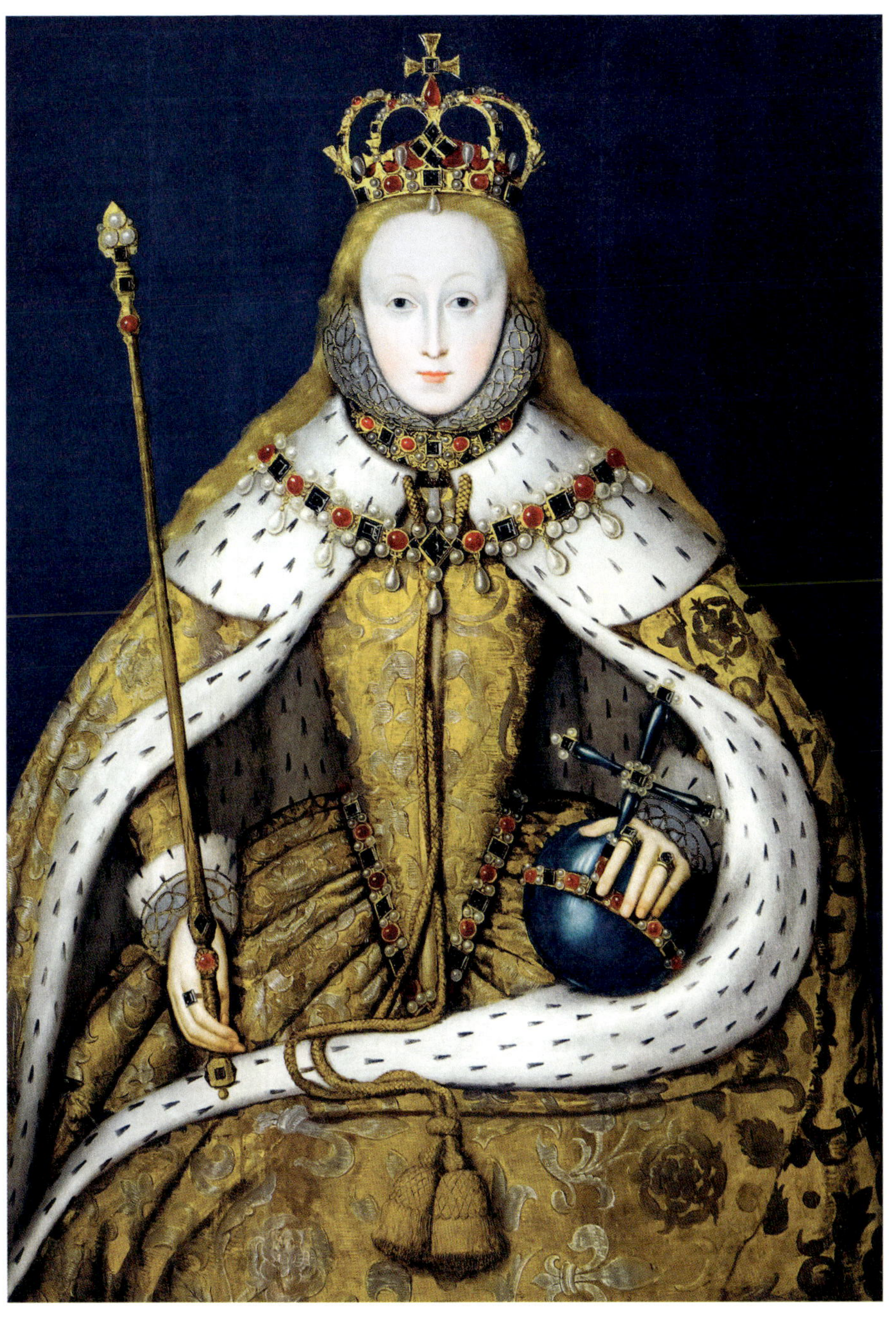

The viewer is probably not intended to see this as a portrait, but as a depiction of Elizabeth's position as Queen of England, in spectacular gold coronation robes.

in January 1559. Elizabeth was not fond of her older sister, who at one time placed her in fear of her life, so the choice to wear her sister's coronation robes might seem surprising.

The re-using of royal garments was common for reasons of tradition and economy – but these were clothes of special significance to Mary and for Elizabeth to wear them at her own coronation was perhaps symbolic. It allowed her to exorcise her sister's ghost and to finally triumph over her regal predecessor. This psychology has a precedent in the Protestant reformers in England, who would re-use Catholic altar clothes and vestments and turn them into domestic furnishings, rather than disposing of them altogether. It was a way of reversing their mysticism and neutralising their power.

Elizabeth was taller and slimmer than Mary, so alterations to the robe were necessary. A new bodice and pair of sleeves were made and 'four yards of Clothe of Tishewe the ground silver, and tyshewe silver' at £4 per yard were delivered for the alterations. The cloth of gold is woven with a pattern of Tudor roses and fleurs-de-lys. Since the 1485 triumph of Henry of Lancaster at the battle of Bosworth, and his union with Elizabeth of York, the Tudor rose was immediately recognisable as the emblem of their dynasty. The lilies refer to the English claim to the French throne.

After Elizabeth's coronation, these sumptuous clothes were once again placed in storage and records reveal that in 1571 the ermine fur of the cloak was repaired by Adam Bland, the Queen's skinner. During its time in store, the fur may have been attacked by moths or, more likely, lost hair around the join of the skins. The garments appear once again in an inventory of the Wardrobe of Robes in 1600, the year this portrait is thought to have been painted.

There is confusion as to whether the fur was ermine or minever (the white winter coat of the red squirrel) but this is most likely an error by the scribe, because historically, ermine has always been used for royal gowns. Ermine is the white winter pelt of a stoat, when only the tip of its tail remains black. Each black ermine tail in this robe therefore denotes the pelt of one animal, with more than two hundred tails to be counted on the visible part of this robe.

The young Queen would surely have commissioned a portrait to commemorate her coronation and this panel is thought to be a copy of a lost original. However, other suggestions have been put forward. Following the coronation, Elizabeth's accession date – 17 November – became a day of commemoration when, each year, church bells rang and festivities took place. This picture may have been painted to commemorate one of these celebrations, or it may have been produced for the Queen's funeral in 1603. Until documentary evidence comes to light, all of the above are conjectural.

Most paintings produced in the early reign of Elizabeth were portraits, primarily likenesses of men and some of women, but few images of individual children. Until the later part of Elizabeth's reign, portraits were generally painted on wooden panels. The wood was primed and given a smooth and even surface that was perfectly suited to the painting of intricate details like the elaborate jewels, smooth silk fabrics and delicate lace ruffs that we see here and which were so typical of the period. The most common panel used in England was fashioned from oak, and the most highly sought-after oak panels were imported from the Eastern Baltic (today's Poland, Lithuania, Latvia and Estonia). Native English oak was available, but it generally produced an uneven, twisted grain that was difficult to cut and finish into the thin, regular-sized boards that were suitable for painting. Panels made from English oak were therefore cheaper to buy and tended to be used by less accomplished artists or by those living a distance from London where supplies of quality materials were limited. The uneven texture of oak panels grown in England was due to the fluctuating temperatures. Boards from trees in the Baltic region had grown in cold, even temperatures where the wood grew slowly, causing the tree rings to be evenly spaced and close together, making for a stable board.

Modern dating techniques use the position of the tree rings to give an approximate date for when the tree was felled and the region in which it grew. This is helpful in ascertaining the authenticity of a work. For example, this painting has been examined using dendrochronology and the results prove that its wooden panel dates to after 1589. It cannot, therefore, be a contemporary portrait of Elizabeth's coronation because, at the time, the tree from which the panel was made was still growing. Once cut and shaped, the panel was seasoned and then prepared for painting. Elizabeth was around 67 and had been Queen for over forty years at the earliest date this painting could have been produced.

Elizabeth's orb and sceptre do not appear in a 1574 inventory of jewels and plate and may have been separately housed in the Jewel House at Whitehall. With its cross mounted on a globe, the orb symbolises the Christian world. It is decorated at the ends and centre with jewels surrounded by pearls. The sceptre represents the monarch's care and control of her people and it matches the rubies, sapphires and pearls that Elizabeth is wearing.

Three crowns were used in the Tudor coronation ceremony. Firstly, St Edward's Crown was placed on the sovereign's head; this was then removed and replaced with the Imperial Crown; and lastly a crown made specifically for the new monarch. Three crowns were prepared by the Jewel House for Elizabeth but, regrettably, nothing remains of the regalia shown in this portrait. After the abolition of the monarchy in 1649, following the English Civil War, the precious stones were prised from their settings and sold, and the gold frames of the crowns were melted down at the royal mint within the Tower of London and turned into coins stamped 'Commonwealth of England'.

Before 1600, there is little known about the display of paintings in England, but most English picture frames were made of a flat panel of oak. We do know that this picture of Elizabeth has received at least three different frames during its lifetime. It was formerly at Warwick Castle where it was displayed in a later, quite grand painted frame. Photographs taken in 1866 can today be viewed in the V&A Museum archives in London and they show this painting in a Sunderland frame likely to have been given to it in the 1670s or 1680s.

The Sunderland frame takes its name from Robert Spencer, 2nd Earl of Sunderland and an ancestor of Diana, Princess of Wales. Between 1665 and 1668, the Earl reframed his extensive collection of paintings at Althorp in gold, baroque-style frames, creating a nationwide fashion that was replicated for the Coronation Portrait at Warwick.

Following a fire at Warwick Castle in 1871, Elizabeth's Coronation Portrait received a third new frame and was hung in the Great Hall at Warwick. It was a heavier and grander frame in the Sansovino style that had been popular in Venice in the 1600s and which saw a resurgence of popularity in England during the late nineteenth century. It is made of a rich dark wood, highlighted with gold, and incorporates garlands of fruit, leaves and grotesque masks.

It is worth noting that, possibly due to the influence of digital presentations, unframed pictures have today become an everyday occurrence. And yet, the choice of frame can dramatically alter the way a painting is viewed. Black frames will emphasise the white in a picture and gold will enhance the blue. In addition to celebrating the glory of God, a gold frame was particularly popular during the Renaissance as it enhanced the traditional blue robes of the Virgin.

Frames are part of the furniture of a room and are often chosen to complement the décor. Once a painting is removed from the room, it is not uncommon to notice that the frame enhanced the room better than the painting contained within it. Of almost 2,700 paintings in the National Gallery, no more than a handful are in their original frames.

When the National Portrait Gallery received this picture, its gilded pine frame was reduced in size at the top and bottom and then refurbished using gesso (traditionally a mixture of animal glue and chalk) as a base for the regilding. It was finally finished and placed on view in 1978. Elizabeth had at last found a permanent home in London.

RELIGION

'There is only one Christ, Jesus, one faith. All else is a dispute over trifles.'

Elizabeth I

Since Henry VIII's break from Rome, the people of England had endured a quarter-century of violent Reformation and Counter-Reformation, based on the personal beliefs of their monarchs. The traditional narrative of the Marian years is one of disasters: flooding, bad harvests, famine and the loss of Calais to the French. But nothing has given Mary a worse reputation than the fires of Smithfield. Nearly 300 Protestants are known to have perished at the stake and their deaths were recorded by John Foxe in his *Acts and Monuments*, commonly known as *Foxe's Book of Martyrs*. Foxe was an ordained Anglican priest whose Puritan beliefs forced him and his pregnant wife into exile, just ahead of officers sent to arrest him. This book, with brutal woodcuts of executions, was hugely influential in shaping English popular opinion against the Catholic Church.

Religion was of fundamental importance and it would now be the most pressing issue of Queen Elizabeth's first Parliament. A restoration of Protestantism was widely anticipated, for Elizabeth was committed to the new faith. In March 1559 she told Feria, the Spanish ambassador, that she 'resolved to restore religion as her father left it'. As the Queen was herself a direct product of the break from Rome, she was bound to reject the Pope, but otherwise her beliefs were not radical. By Calvinist standards she was a conservative who, like her father, enjoyed the traditional ceremonies of religion. Her chaplains wore splendid, embroidered robes, the crucifix was displayed and she listened to glorious anthems and motets (short pieces of sacred choral music) sung by choristers. She liked candles, stained glass and colourful images and she disliked married clergy.

In an age when people were burned for their beliefs, Elizabeth held surprisingly tolerant views and hated fanaticism. She told the French ambassador, André Hurault, 'There is only one Christ, Jesus, one faith. All else is a dispute over trifles.' Her religious policy would be an attempt to unite her divided country and she had already decided that it must be Protestant, with elements of Catholic rituals.

Elizabeth's settlement comprised two Acts of Parliament, passed in 1559: The Act of Supremacy and The Act of Uniformity. The former made Elizabeth the Supreme Governor of the Church of England and the latter reintroduced the Book of Common Prayer. Thus, the Catholic Church lost its authority in England, for the second time, and Anglican worship was once again established in the nation's churches.

For her Archbishop of Canterbury, Elizabeth chose Matthew Parker. A moderate man, he had also once been the chaplain of her mother, Anne Boleyn. Parker gave the people the Bishops' Bible, an English translation published at his own expense in 1572, and his influence would help Anglican theology take shape.

Elizabeth believed that a moderate Church of England, not so different from the old faith, would gradually woo her subjects away from Catholicism. She was largely right and by the end of her reign most people accepted this hybrid of Protestant liturgy with Catholic traditions. The Church of England's character today is still the result of this Elizabethan Settlement.

There was broad support for the new Church and very few refused to take the oath of allegiance to the Queen. She asked for outward conformity to her laws on religion but, according to the writer and philosopher Francis Bacon, had 'no desire to make windows into men's souls'. Providing her subjects were loyal to herself and the state, Elizabeth was content, but this approach did not please everyone. Her reign would later become notorious for the persecution of Catholics, though this was born of political necessity and not religious fanaticism on her part. Opposition also came from extreme Protestants, known as Puritans, who wanted to 'purify' the Church of all residue of the Catholic faith. Many Puritans had fled abroad when Mary was queen, but returned to Elizabeth's England. They raised their views in Parliament, but did not seek to overthrow the regime and were therefore less of a threat than Catholics. Some of Elizabeth's most trusted advisors, notably Robert Dudley and Sir Francis Walsingham, were Puritans in the sense of seeking to extinguish Catholic traditions. But Elizabeth firmly resisted their attempts to change her Religious Settlement. The Queen would later quash a number of Puritan bills, such as the call for prohibition of sports and entertainments on Sundays and the move to make heresy and blasphemy criminal offences. English Puritans also wanted to remove sacred music from churches, just as it had been swept away in Reformation Scotland. Their efforts were in vain, for this was a much-loved Catholic practice that Elizabeth was determined to protect.

GOD'S MUSIC

Music was a vital component of church worship before the Reformation and it was essential for Henry VIII to have a highly trained chapel choir who could sing in Latin to the glory of God and the King. Edward VI was fond of music, but the radical Protestantism of his reign meant choirs were generally disbanded and church organs destroyed. Where church music did survive it took the form of a sermon, sung not in Latin but in simple English – clearly heard and understood. Under Queen Mary's Catholicism, the old style of music returned to the chapels and then, with Elizabeth, the stage was set for a new golden age of choral arrangements.

Music was a lifelong passion for Elizabeth I. Her tutor, Roger Ascham, said in 1550, 'She is as much delighted with music as she is skilful in the art.' She was accomplished on the lute, a stringed instrument favoured by her father, Henry VIII, and her singing voice was praised. As Queen, she employed over 70 musicians, and names like Thomas Tallis and William Byrd would go on to become the most influential composers of the sixteenth century. The virginals, a keyboard instrument of the harpsichord family, seems to have been her favourite instrument and she spent hours practising. One of Elizabeth's virginals, dated from a tiny inscription to 1594 and bearing the Boleyn arms, is now housed in the Victoria & Albert Museum in London. The Queen claimed on one occasion to have composed dance music, although no compositions by her have so far been discovered. Her love of music was so well known that on her deathbed musicians were summoned to comfort the Queen and revive her.

In 1564, when informed by the Scottish envoy, Sir James Melville, that Mary, Queen of Scots, played both lute and virginals, Elizabeth wondered how well Mary played. Later that day, Melville was asked by an English courtier to listen to some music and taken to a gallery where he heard a melody that 'ravished him'. The player turned out to be Elizabeth herself and she disingenuously told Melville that she had not been expecting him. However, since he had now heard her, perhaps he could judge whether her playing or that of the Scottish Queen was better? Melville was obliged to answer that Elizabeth was the superior musician.

Elizabeth I of England Playing the Lute

Nicholas Hilliard, c. 1576/80, portrait miniature, vellum stuck onto card, Berkeley Castle, Gloucestershire

Although Elizabeth I was praised as an accomplished lute player, this portrait is unlikely to have been taken from life. The miniature probably hails from the collection of the Queen's cousin Henry Carey, 1st Baron Hunsdon, its provenance coming through his granddaughter Elizabeth, wife of Sir Thomas Berkeley. It can be considered both an icon suggesting the harmony of the body politic and a reference to the musical interests of the Carey family. Henry Carey was patron of the Chamberlain's Men, Shakespeare's company of actors, and a supporter of the accomplished lutist and composer John Dowland.

Dowland's *First Book of Songs* was published in 1597 and uncommonly includes a piece of music written for two players on one lute. It became one of the most influential collections of music in the history of the instrument and it may have been the Carey family's interest in the lute that prompted them to commission this portrait.

It is only the second picture of a Tudor monarch playing a musical instrument, the first being a miniature of Henry VIII playing the harp (from a book of Psalms belonging to the King, now held in the British Library). The delicate detail of the gold edging and the fretwork on the lute indicate that it was most likely painted through observation of an actual instrument because even the grain of the wood can be discerned. The neck of the lute is longer than those of Italian lutes depicted in the art of the period and so it may have been an English creation.

In relation to the throne behind her, the Queen's body is strangely twisted and it is difficult to discern if she is sitting or standing. However, she appears relaxed, with the position of her hands credible as those of a musician, albeit with improbably elongated fingers. On either side of the throne is a crowned pomegranate, which refers to queenship, fertility and the Resurrection of Christ. They were introduced into Tudor symbolism by Katherine of Aragon and deployed by both Mary I and Elizabeth. The fruits are curiously shaded in such a manner as to resemble two eyes, with the Queen seated between them, and although probably not intentional, once seen, their placing is imposing and difficult to ignore. The composition, including the elaborate and fantastic throne, is reminiscent of manuscript painting, from where miniatures in England first took their inspiration during the reign of Elizabeth's father, Henry VIII.

The elaborate costume, with its jewels and embroidered sleeves, echoes a dress worn by Elizabeth in a portrait at Reading Museum, Berkshire, and may suggest a date of around 1575, before Hilliard went to France, although other estimates place this miniature in the 1580s.

The painting has suffered somewhat from the oxidation of the silver used on Elizabeth's dress, which originally would have shimmered against the chair upholstered in black and trimmed with gold. This miniature is one of very few English pictures of a lute at a time when it was at the centre of musical life. The Queen's face is unfortunately damaged and the background, the throne and the inlaid table in the foreground are flatly painted, leaving the starring role in this portrait to the lute itself.

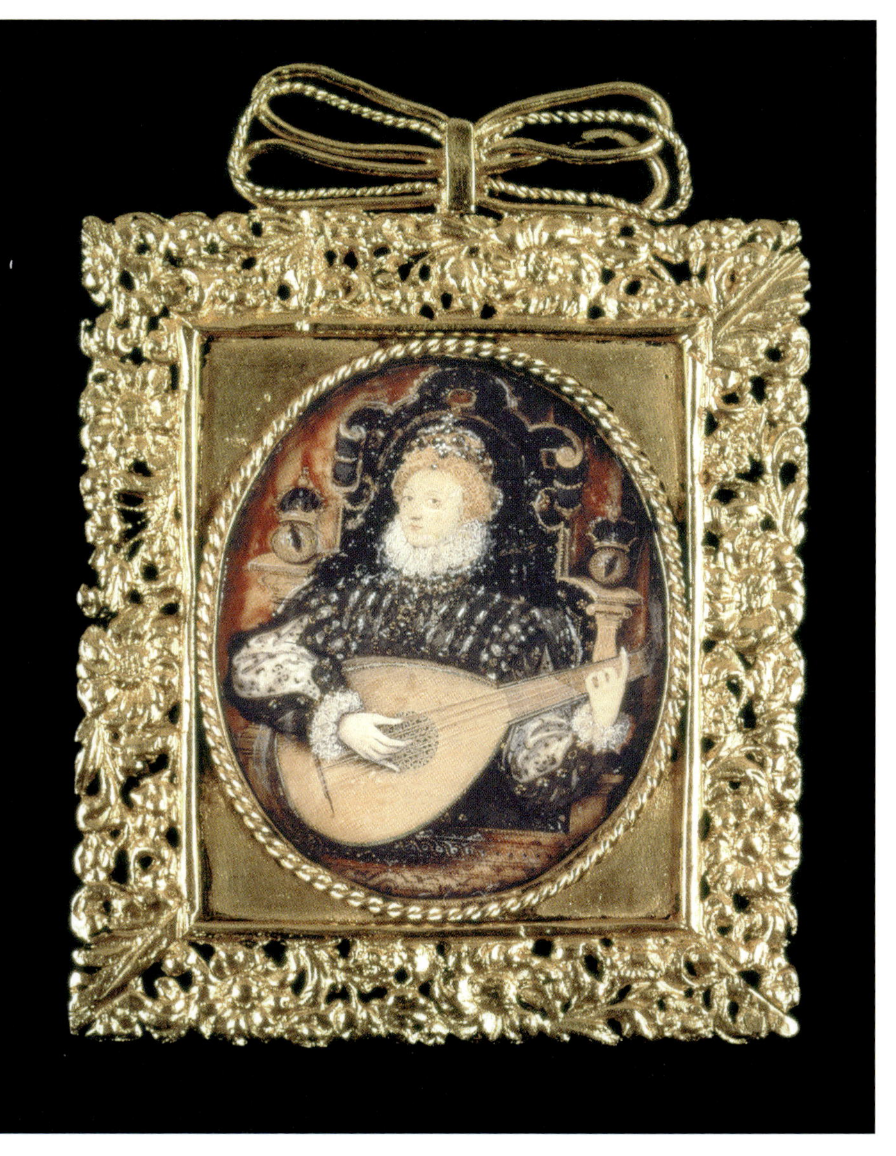

Music was a lifelong passion for Elizabeth, as it was for her father. She was an accomplished player of the lute (shown here) and virginals.

In Elizabeth's England music was so highly regarded that most noblemen employed their own musicians. Gentleman were also expected to sing and to read music, which was printed and readily available from booksellers. Its significance in the culture of the time was echoed in the plays of William Shakespeare, who makes more than 500 references to music in his works. Elizabethan music was known for its steady rhythm and its polyphony, where songs sung often included a four-to-five-part harmony with multiple melodies weaving throughout one another.

This very spiritual art form would find deeper, intoxicating expression in Elizabeth's chapels, where it is described as choral polyphony. It can be heard in the new service of Evensong, which was created around 1549, as part of the English Reformation. The liturgy of Evensong comes from Archbishop Thomas Cranmer's *Book of Common Prayer* and is sung in harmony at the even point between day and night. The whole idea is derived from monastic prayer traditions and Elizabeth's melodic Evensong is unchanged to this day.

English composers such as Thomas Tallis lived and worked through the religious changes of four monarchs and had to be flexible, changing content and writing masterpieces in English as well as Latin. Tallis was 54 when Elizabeth became queen and he adjusted his style for what would be the last time. His better-known works are Elizabethan, including the motet '*Spem in alium*', written for eight five-voice choirs, but several of his anthems written during Edward's reign are judged to be on the same level, such as 'If Ye Love Me'. He would live to be 80 years old. As a Catholic in dangerous times, his deep faith was never written down but is vividly demonstrated in his music.

Other accomplished musicians included Orlando Gibbons, John Taverner, John Dowland, Christopher Tye and Tallis's pupil William Byrd – one of the great masters of European Renaissance music. All these composers were able to create a sense of the divine, in Latin and English, through works of incredible serenity. Their music glorified not only God but the monarchy too. It was both an ornament and a form of power which would impress visitors from Europe. Many composers who wrote for the Church also wrote for court and came to exemplify the era with their beautiful arrangements.

Music continued to flourish under the Queen's patronage and in 1575 she granted Tallis and Byrd exclusive rights for the importing, printing, publishing and sale of music. The two friends and colleagues went on to publish a collection of vocal sacred music, *Cantiones sacrae*, which they dedicated to Elizabeth. During this time, William Byrd was a gentleman of the Chapel Royal, where he shared the duties of organist with Tallis, and produced secular and sacred compositions for the Queen. He was also associating with prominent Catholics and at one point his house was searched for priests, resulting in his temporary suspension from the Chapel Royal. Though Byrd was often cited as a Catholic and had to pay fines, he was considered loyal to the Crown and was protected from severe punishment by the Queen. Like Tallis, he lived to a great age and his death, in 1623, was noted in the Chapel Royal, describing him as 'a Father of Musick'.

Sacred music was unacceptable to radical Protestants, who saw it as a distraction from the Word of God. They discouraged polyphony, unless the words were clearly audible, and they tried to remove Evensong and the use of church organs altogether. But the Queen continued to love and defend sacred music against the Puritans of her realm and she ensured its survival. Through the compositions of Elizabeth's talented musicians, the vaulted roofs of her churches echoed to the most astonishing beauty, perhaps transcending the bitter conflicts of religious beliefs.

4

'ONE MISTRESS AND NO MASTER': MARRIAGE GAME

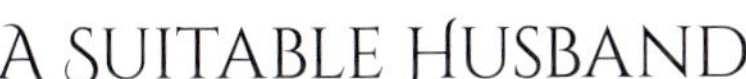

A SUITABLE HUSBAND

Elizabeth was only 25 when she became queen, so everyone expected her to make a favourable match and provide an heir to her throne. Unmarried female monarchs were unheard of, but ultimately the most eligible bride in Europe chose to remain single. It is worth noting that she was the first English monarch in 500 years who did not try to produce a legitimate successor. The Queen caused political uncertainty by refusing to marry – or even nominate an heir from possible candidates – and there has been considerable speculation as to her reasons.

Events from Elizabeth's childhood may have put her off the very idea of marriage. Henry VIII had executed two of his wives: Elizabeth's mother Anne Boleyn and her stepmother Catherine Howard. Then, Elizabeth's first experience of sexual attraction, with Thomas Seymour when she was 14, had been traumatic. There was another danger associated with marriage: two of the Queen's stepmothers, Jane Seymour and Katherine Parr, and her grandmother, Elizabeth of York, had died in childbirth. It was the greatest danger a woman could face, with no antiseptics or modern pain relief. Even queens could die, despite having access to the best doctors and medicines, so it would be unsurprising if Elizabeth feared childbirth, despite the pressing need for an heir.

But political reasons were even more compelling than any psychological or physical fears. A match with a European prince, who would enhance her royal status, might also draw England into foreign wars, and the most eligible princes were all Catholics. However, marrying an Englishman would mean a union beneath her rank and it would cause jealousy, as he would inevitably promote his own family to wealth and influence.

Not only was the Queen reluctant to commit herself to any man but her council of advisors was also always divided on the matter. They would regularly entreat Elizabeth to provide an heir but they could never agree on a suitable husband. Both Queen and council had also witnessed the political difficulties of Mary I and Mary, Queen of Scots, both of whom encountered rebellion as a result of their choice of husbands. It even cost the Scottish queen her throne.

Furthermore, in the sixteenth century a husband was deemed to have authority over his wife and marriage might bring some erosion of Elizabeth's power. As early as

1564, the Scottish ambassador, Sir James Melville, judged correctly, saying, 'You will never marry … the Queen of England is too proud to suffer a commander … you think if you were married, you would only be Queen of England, and now you are king and queen both.'

Queen Elizabeth I (The Darnley Portrait)

Unknown continental artist, c. 1575, oil on panel, National Portrait Gallery, London

The 'Darnley Portrait' of Elizabeth I, so called because it used to belong to the Earls of Darnley, is one of the key images of the Queen. It is an accomplished work, showing us the real woman with all her power, determination and composure.

She wears a rich, Polish-style doublet with a lace ruff collar; a double string of pearls is looped around her neck and she holds an ostrich-feather fan. The ruff, a fashion accessory that came to define the Elizabethan era, was a circular collar made from a pleated frill. It was worn by both men and women, aristocrats and proletarians alike, but the quality of material varied greatly, from very expensive fine linens to cheap fabric for poorer folk. These collars became increasingly outlandish as time passed. The small ruff at Elizabeth's neck here would grow in size until it formed the huge, detachable cart-wheel ruff at its most extreme in the 1580s.

This image is more lifelike than later portraits, as it resulted from a sitting, possibly the last time Elizabeth posed for an artist. The resulting face pattern was used for many years, suggesting that she approved of the likeness. Elizabeth and her council realised that her image was a powerful political tool and a proclamation had been passed in 1563 to regulate its production. The proposal included creating a pattern for use by painters and engravers across the country, preserving the impression of flawless beauty. While the artist of this portrait is unrecorded, the sophisticated and swiftly rendered paint suggests a foreign painter, possibly from the Netherlands.

The crown and sceptre on a table beside the Queen mark the first appearance of these symbols being used as props (rather than worn or carried) in Tudor portraiture, a theme that would recur in later portraits. They were probably added right at the end, at the request of the patron, and are the work of a different, less competent artist. This is evidenced by the difference in the delicate paint handling of her dress, for example, in contrast to the methodical use of paint to depict the crown.

Technical analysis shows a drawing, beneath the paint, which evolved as the artist worked. The paint is freely handled, with wet-in-wet blending, in which fresh paint is layered over paint that is not completely dry, a technique indicating the high skill and mastery of the artist. English artists at this time tended to wait for one layer of paint to dry before adding another. We can see this wet-in-wet blending most clearly in Elizabeth's fixed fan of colourful and exotic feathers, set into a handle.

Whoever commissioned the work (probably a courtier close to the Queen) may have given her the fan or the jewelled pendant hanging from her waist. These items are prominent in the painting and, to those in the know, would symbolise a familiar relationship between monarch and subject. Everyone at court offered gifts to the Queen at New Year and there are records of luxurious fans being presented, such as the one given by Dudley at New Year 1574. Frustratingly, none of the descriptions exactly match

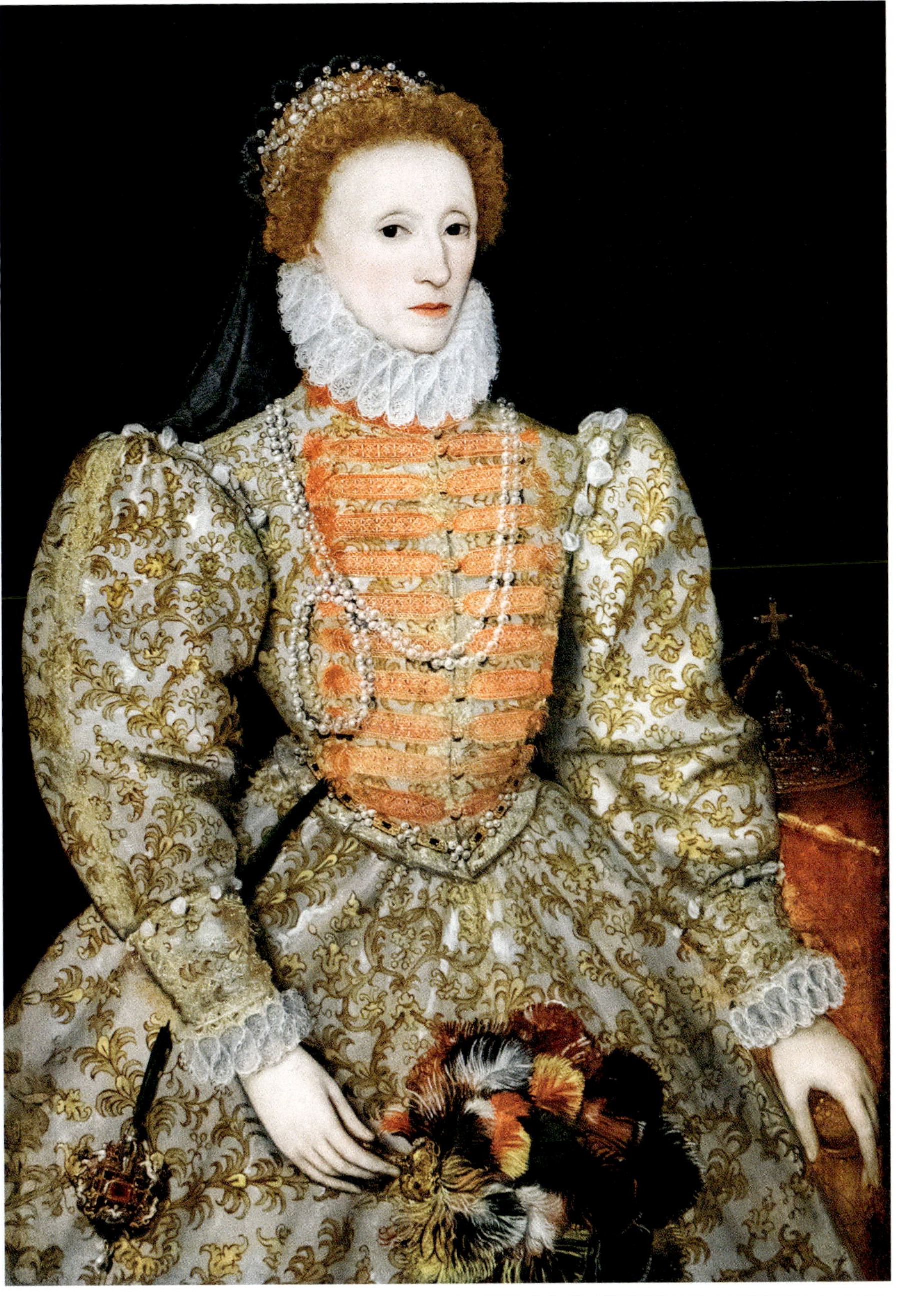

The Darnley Portrait from 1575 was possibly the last time Elizabeth posed for an artist. The face pattern was used for many years afterwards.

the item in this portrait, so they cannot help us identify the patron. The large pendant is typical of the Renaissance jewels often gifted to Elizabeth by her many suitors. This one comprises a large red ruby, surrounded by Roman deities such as Minerva and Neptune. Minerva is an entirely appropriate motif for Elizabeth, being a virgin and fighter for just causes who was also renowned for promoting peace.

Conservation work has revealed that the red pigment in the flesh tones has faded over time, giving Elizabeth a much paler appearance than originally intended. Her face was once rosier and more natural and her crimson gown was far richer in colour. The borders of the golden-brown pattern may have originally been a reddish purple, a change caused by the instability of the blue pigment 'smalt' as well as the fading of red lake. (Lake pigments are organic and not lightfast; they were often used during the Renaissance as translucent glazes to enhance the colours of rich fabrics and draperies.)

A reproduction of this dress was made in 1971 for the acclaimed BBC miniseries *Elizabeth R*. Costume designer Elizabeth Waller recreated a number of other gowns from official portraits, including the Armada and Ditchley outfits, and won an Emmy award for her work. The actor Glenda Jackson wore complex make-up to portray Elizabeth from a young princess to a wrinkled monarch; she even had her head partially shaved to achieve an extremely high hairline. Getting Jackson dressed was time-consuming and required considerable help, just as it would have done in the sixteenth century. Jean Hunnisett, the costumer who made the gowns, stated in her book *Period Costume for Stage & Screen: Patterns for Women's Dress 1500–1800* that 'the whole operation of dressing Miss Jackson, including a full wig change, took four people about 20 minutes'.

'SWEET ROBIN'

There is no doubt that Elizabeth was attracted to hand-some, charismatic men and during her reign she revelled in the flattery of a succession of courtiers including Christopher Hatton, Walter Raleigh and later Robert Devereux, Earl of Essex. But Robert Dudley, Earl of Leicester, was probably her greatest love.

The story of Elizabeth and Dudley has fascinated people for centuries and their relationship has been explored in books, films and television. They were the same age and had known each other since childhood. On becoming queen, she appointed him Master of the Horse – a great officer of the Royal Household. It meant responsibility for overseeing royal progresses, riding and hunting together almost daily and much personal contact.

Dudley was tall and handsome, loved music and the arts and was equally accomplished in dancing and joust-ing. In short, he was everything that Elizabeth found attractive in a man. He also had the ability to entertain her: they enjoyed sharing private jokes and teasing each other. Elizabeth often bestowed pet names and Robert became 'Sweet Robin' and her 'Eyes'. They would play on the latter by drawing double 'o's as eyes in their fre-quent correspondence. The relationship could be stormy at times, when Dudley overstretched his power or became petulant. During one argument, prompted by his jealousy of another courtier, Elizabeth angrily declared, 'I will have here but one mistress, and no master.' However, Robert was soon forgiven.

The attraction between them was so obvious that it gave rise to gossip at home and abroad. Philip of Spain was informed that 'Lord Robert has come so much into favour that he does whatever he likes with affairs and it is even said that her majesty visits him in his chamber day and night'. Many diplomats related that Elizabeth was enamoured of him – but Robert Dudley was already married. Rumours spread that the Queen would wed him if she could and then, in 1560, his wife Amy died by falling downstairs and breaking her neck. The circumstances were suspicious and a scandal ensued. William Cecil had long despaired that a Dudley match would bring ruin to the Queen and he was not alone. Kat Ashley, who had been Elizabeth's devoted governess, begged her mistress to desist from her public display of affection. Robert had supported his father's attempt to place Lady Jane Grey on the throne and the family were tainted by treason. Although they had returned to royal favour, the fact remained that both his father John and grandfather Edmund had been beheaded on Tower Hill. Historians have generally concluded that Robert was not involved in Amy's death but, at the time, the damage was done. Coupled with the unpopularity of the Dudley family, it meant that Elizabeth could never marry him.

There has always been speculation on the possible sexual nature of the Dudley relationship, but it is highly unlikely that Elizabeth would have risked her throne by sleeping with her favourite. What is certain is that she wanted him by her side and trusted him completely. In 1562, the Queen contracted smallpox and it is a testament to her faith in Dudley that she requested he be made Lord Protector of England, should she die. After her recovery he was appointed to the Privy Council, gifted Kenilworth Castle in 1563 and elevated to Earl of Leicester in 1564. It's clear he was not just an ornament of court, but a leading and influential figure in the Elizabethan administration, working alongside William Cecil. In the end, Robert Dudley and the

Queen were close friends for more than thirty years and she was extremely jealous of his affections. Her love brought him fame, titles and power but, despite his best efforts, he would never achieve the ultimate prize of making Elizabeth his wife.

Robert Dudley, 1st Earl of Leicester

Unknown Anglo-Netherlandish artist, c. 1575, oil on panel, National Portrait Gallery, London

In this portrait, the 43-year-old Dudley wears a hugely expensive red silk or satin suit, finely embroidered with gold thread, and a jewelled hat with matching red feather. The badge of the Order of the Garter, which he joined in 1559, can be seen hanging from his neck and again in the background, enclosing his coat of arms and topped with his Earl's coronet.

His doublet (jacket) is fashionably tight-fitting to accentuate his shape. It is padded above the waistline (like a pea in a pod) and extends lower than the natural waist, dipping down to a point at the front. Known as a 'peascod' doublet, it was viewed as a projection of masculinity, in a similar way to the codpiece in portraits of Henry VIII. It is matched with pumpkin-shaped trunk-hose, stiffened and padded with bombast (stuffing of cotton or horsehair) and constructed in slashed panes of fabric to reveal a contrasting silk underneath. In 1562, this flamboyant and extravagant fashion was the subject of sumptuary legislation that regulated its volume and the amount of fabric used in its construction.

As Elizabeth's reign progressed, so hose became much shorter, revealing shapely limbs clad in brightly coloured stockings. This portrait may originally have depicted Dudley full-length, allowing for the display of his comely legs, but most likely due to woodworm, the panel has been cut down. For an Elizabethan gentleman, the ideal leg to aspire to would be lean, muscular and elongated, as shown in the background of the Sieve Portrait (fig. 9). However, although the knitted silk stockings had some stretch, it is unlikely that the wrinkle-free depiction of male legs in Tudor portraiture reflected reality.

The sleeves were detachable, padded and often decorated with an embroidered pattern, as seen in this case at the wrist. There is 'pinking' (decorative cuts) on the surface of his doublet and it is further embellished with twenty gold buttons. Gold buttons were considered a masculine feature and an expensive item of display.

Although stylish, the Earl's high ruff would have restricted his ability to turn his head, requiring a turn of the whole body, and the tight doublet inhibited turning at the waist. The result would have been a very mannered style of movement, indicating the wearer's high status in clothes unsuited to any kind of physical labour and looking unnatural, restrictive and highly uncomfortable. The ideal male silhouette of this period had hips as well as a waist and appeared oddly curvaceous.

Such high-standing collars and large ruffs were accompanied by shorter hair for men, so as not to interfere with the neckline. The Earl's hair is here brushed upwards at the forehead, which suited the popular crowned hat of the period.

This panel has been constructed from three panels of high-quality Eastern Baltic oak taken from a tree felled between 1568 and 1579. In conjunction with the fashions described above and noting Dudley's moustache and beard, which are precisely trimmed in keeping with

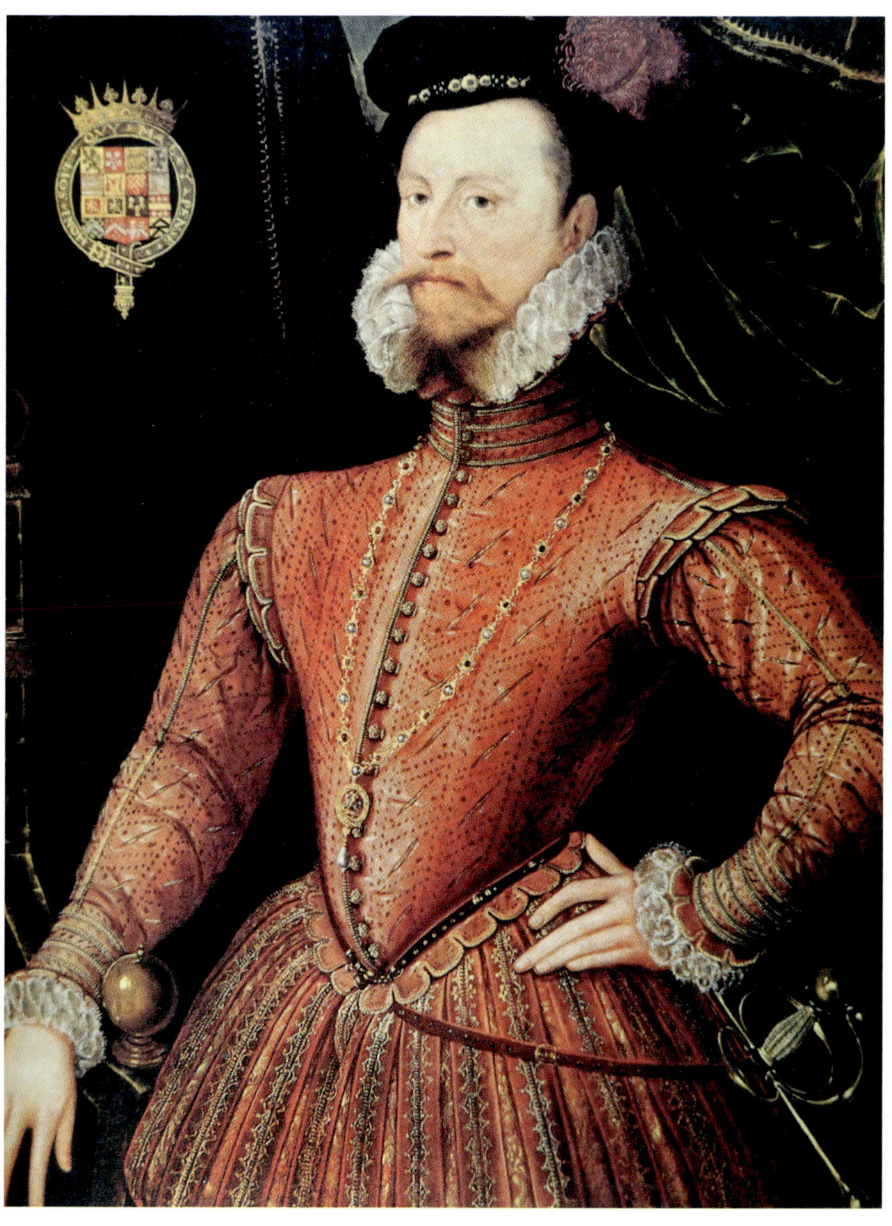

Robert Dudley was interested in his own image and how it could be used to spectacular effect, furthering his cause to marry the Queen.

1570s fashion, this confirms the attributed date of *c.* 1575. Infrared technology reveals extensive under-drawing and tracing, suggesting that Robert Dudley's image was initially taken from a pattern and then built up in freehand once transferred to the panel. Interestingly, the artist's preparatory drawing, produced almost 500 years ago, is today revealed to the naked eye through the thinning surface of the paint.

This may be the portrait listed in Dudley's inventory at Kenilworth Castle, in which he is described as wearing 'a sute of russet satten and velvet welted' and which is associated with Elizabeth's visit there in 1575. The occasion was his last desperate and spectacular attempt to persuade Elizabeth to marry him. Sparing no expense, he invited her to Kenilworth, on his Warwickshire estate, and staged weeks of extraordinarily lavish entertainments at a huge cost.

Most Elizabethan courtiers sat for their portraits infrequently. Even among foreign rulers, few commissioned as many paintings of themselves as Robert Dudley, of whom at least twenty are known, although there were probably more. A reasonable number still exist, notably at the National Portrait Gallery, the Wallace Collection and Waddesdon Manor. There was also a demand for copies of his portrait, a version of which survives in the collection at Hatfield House, Hertfordshire, as evidence that it was disseminated. The Earl was good-looking and vain, but this was not the only reason for all his self-portraits. In common with Elizabeth, he was particularly interested in his own image and how it could be used, along with clothing, to spectacular effect – in his case, furthering his cause to marry the Queen by depicting a handsome, virile nobleman who aspired to match with her. The pose of this portrait also lends it to being hung as a pair, with a possible 'pendant' picture of Elizabeth hung side by side, as if they were a couple.

For all Tudor people, clothing was the principal marker of class, an expression of status and identity. The Elizabethan elite favoured complex surface decoration on silks, satins and velvet, which could be padded, slashed and embroidered. For men, dress was more effeminate than in the previous generation. The bulky, layered appearance of Henry VIII's reign, designed to make the male sex look aggressive and dominant, had disappeared and the loose-fitting top gown of Henry's reign, which featured so prominently in his iconic portraits, was now usually replaced by a dashing cloak, typically worn over one shoulder.

In addition to being one of the most influential people at the Elizabethan court, Robert Dudley was also an ardent patron of artists, recognised throughout Europe as the greatest collector in England. In 1574, he persuaded the celebrated Italian Federico Zuccaro to come to England, where the artist completed life-sized portraits of the Queen and Dudley, to be displayed together at Kenilworth. The Earl owned a staggering 200 paintings and, interestingly, he did not take the English view of painters as simply craftsmen but held the Renaissance belief that great artists deserved status. His galleries at Kenilworth, Wanstead Manor and Leicester House, London, included works by Nicholas Hilliard, François Clouet and Paolo Veronese. He collected pictures of various foreign princes and dignitaries; Catherine de' Medici sent him a painting of her son, the Duke of Anjou (who would later become a rival for Elizabeth's hand).

Dudley's executed forbears were not included in the galleries, although he did own portraits of his immediate family such as his nephew Sir Philip Sidney, who acted as his artistic agent in Europe. Unsurprisingly, he commissioned at least seven portraits of Elizabeth, and he set a trend amongst courtiers to have coded references to themselves in their pictures of the Queen. This might take the form of including items of clothing or accessories gifted to Elizabeth by the patron. For those aware of the signs, it would confirm the intimacy of the courtier's relationship with their sovereign.

The Queen and her court were the source of advancement and patronage for ambitious young men. They competed for her favour and Elizabeth played them off against each other, just as she did with foreign suitors, so increasing her own power. Gentlemen wore ever more colourful, extravagant and impractical outfits in their bid to be noticed by the Queen, whether they were dancing or jousting.

As previously mentioned, sitting for a portrait was an infrequent event and the subject's most expensive clothing was worn. This proclaimed the status of the wearer to the contemporary viewer because legislation stated that everyone dressed according to their rank. In practice, these laws were hard to enforce but it is safe to assume that, while an individual might break the rules in everyday life, they would draw the line at having the transgression recorded in paint. Therefore, this elite outfit – and Dudley's right to wear it – is significant. Elizabeth demanded a sense of style and her courtiers spent vast sums on their wardrobes to impress her. It was not uncommon for men to mortgage their estates or sell land to pay mercers and tailors, in the hope of advancement at court. The jealous rivals were encouraged to compete, like colourful, virile peacocks, in elaborate and ever more impractical swagger.

THE MARRIAGE GAME

There was no shortage of eminent suitors to the Queen of England and she was able to use her marriage prospects as a political tool for most of her reign. Elizabeth encouraged and enjoyed the attentions of powerful men such as Philip of Spain, Erik XIV of Sweden, the Archduke Charles of Austria and the Duke of Anjou, who were kept in hope of winning her hand. In this way, England could ensure their friendship, while Elizabeth made a deliberate policy of protracted negotiations, blending romance with diplomacy. If she chose one candidate in the 'marriage game', it would upset the delicate political balance of her foreign policy by alienating his rivals.

THE HAMPDEN PORTRAIT

Steven van der Meulen (or George Gower), c. 1563, oil on canvas transferred to panel, private collection

The first known full-length depiction of England's Queen is thought to have been created expressly for this royal marriage market. *The Hampden Portrait* by Steven van der Meulen was painted in 1563 as a gift from Queen Elizabeth to Griffith Hampden to commemorate her visit to Hampden House and is today in a private collection. It's filled with messages of beauty, fidelity and fertility as Elizabeth is depicted with a background of luscious fruits and flowers. She is clearly young and the image proclaims her marriage potential and ability to bear children. To avoid any doubt, she even holds a sixteenth-century symbol of betrothal and motherly love: the carnation flower. The choice of a red and white dress perhaps signifies the union of York and Lancaster. The red and white Tudor rose was created by combining the emblem of the House of Lancaster (the red rose) with that of the House of York (the white rose). These rival houses were united in 1486 by the marriage of the Lancastrian Henry VII and Elizabeth of York, after years of civil war (the Wars of the Roses). The Tudor rose was used in Elizabeth's portraits to refer to the Tudor dynasty and the unity it brought. The rose also had religious connotations, as the medieval symbol of the Virgin Mary, and here it alludes to Elizabeth as her secular successor.

This message appears again in her Tudor rose collar and her corsage, where the placing of oak leaves, instead of rose leaves, may be a playful reference to Robert Dudley (*quercus robur*, the Latin for English oak, possibly puns on his first name). This early portrait of the Queen is notable for its lifelike depiction of Elizabeth – showing her own hair – before the construction of the bewigged, painted 'goddess' we find in much later portraits. It is a portrait that would have appealed to her princely admirers in their palaces around Europe.

The only foreign suitor to actually visit Elizabeth was the Duke of Anjou, youngest son of Henri II of France, who was 24 when he arrived in 1579. The French prince was short in stature and pockmarked, but must have possessed great charm, for the 46-year-old Queen was soon quite taken with him. She enjoyed being wooed in person by an illustrious suitor, who (of course) declared passionate love for her, and she fondly called him her 'Frog'. The political motive for this match was to form an alliance against Spain but there was much resentment from Robert Dudley, Christopher Hatton and other favourites and – as always – plenty of obstacles in the way.

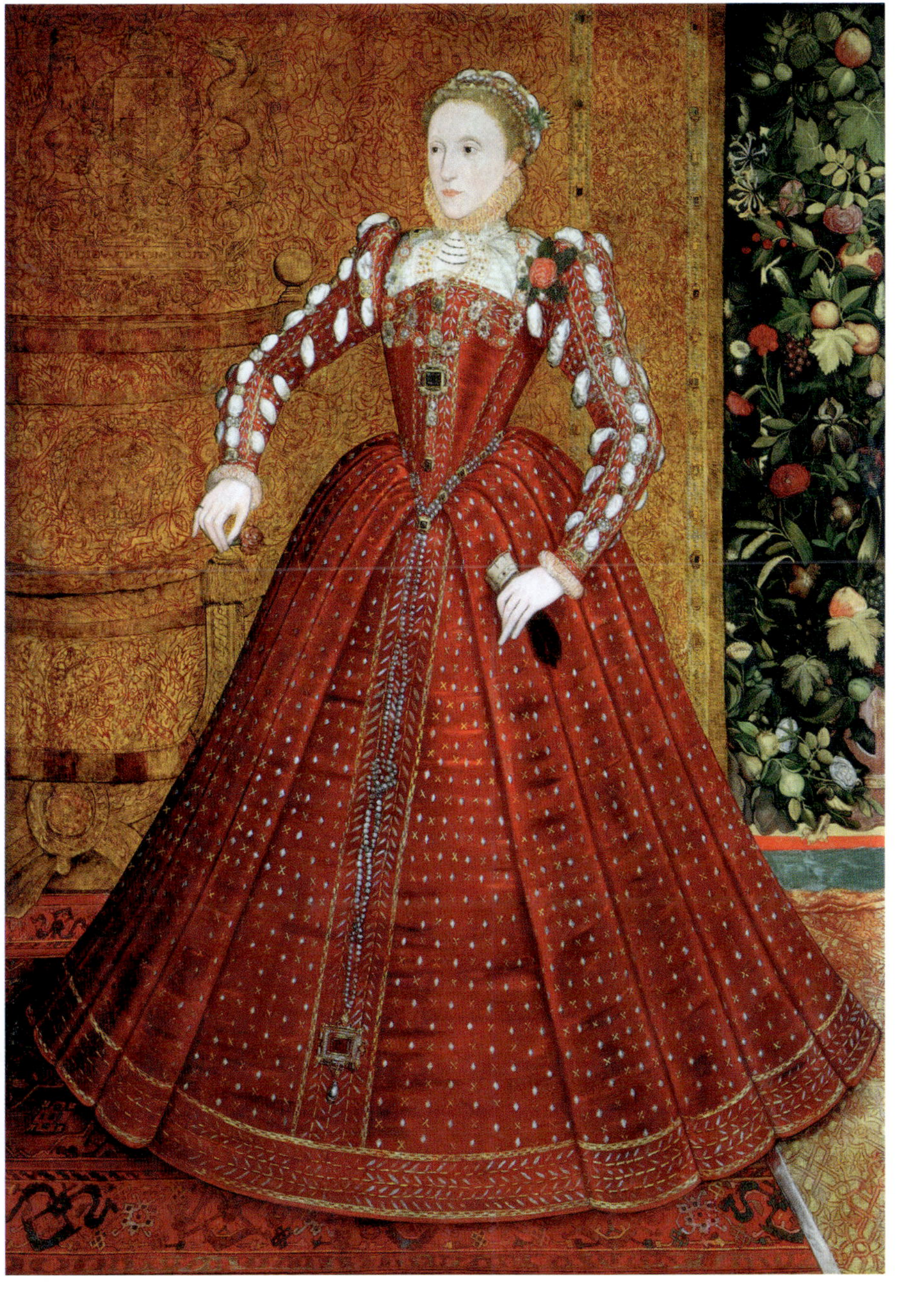

The Hampden Portrait of Elizabeth is notable for its early lifelike depiction and would have appealed to her royal admirers in their palaces around Europe.

Anjou was not only Catholic but heir presumptive to the French throne. The Puritan pamphleteer John Stubbs drew public attention to this 'contrary coupling' and lost his right hand as punishment for incurring the Queen's wrath. Elizabeth and Anjou enjoyed a lengthy courtship but, after strong opposition from the Privy Council, she finally said farewell to her 'Frog'. The poem she penned about him, 'On Monsieur's Departure', demonstrates poetic skill and a true depth of feeling belonging to Elizabeth the mortal woman. It suggests her feelings for Anjou may have been genuine, or perhaps she was lamenting the end of courtship itself, believing him to be her last suitor:

> I grieve and dare not show my discontent;
> I love, and yet am forced to seem to hate;
> I do, yet dare not say I ever meant;
> I seem stark mute, but inwardly do prate.
> I am, and not; I freeze and yet am burned,
> Since from myself another self I turned.

VIRGIN QUEEN

'This shall be for me sufficient, that a marble stone shall declare that a Queen, having reigned such a time, lived and died a virgin.'

Elizabeth I

Elizabeth's Anglican Church largely rejected the Catholic worship of the Virgin Mary and this played to the Queen's advantage; the vacancy was now a position she intended to fill herself and courtly love would be infused with religious veneration. The 'religion' of Elizabeth would see her

'Accession Day' become a national holiday, like a saint's day, celebrated with increased fervour.

At the same time, she promoted her maiden state – a fact that was to form the substance of her legend. The 'Virgin Queen' was portrayed as a selfless woman who sacrificed romantic love and personal happiness for the good of the nation. Elizabeth wore a pelican jewel in several portraits as a symbol of her selfless love for her people. The message would not be lost on contemporary observers; according to legend, the pelican pricked its own breast to feed its children with the blood and save their lives. In the process of feeding, the mother would die. In the Middle Ages the pelican came to represent Jesus sacrificing himself on the cross for the good of mankind and the sacrament of communion, feeding the faithful with his body and blood (see fig. 12).

Was Elizabeth I really a virgin? We have no conclusive proof, one way or another. At home and abroad, rumours about her love life circulated. The King of France joked that one of the great questions of the day was 'whether Queen Elizabeth was a maid or no' and plenty of hostile Catholic sources claimed the Queen was engaged in secret sexual liaisons and had even given birth to illegitimate children.

However, while Elizabeth may have enjoyed some physical intimacy with Robert Dudley, it is unlikely that full sexual intercourse took place. An unplanned pregnancy was simply too great a risk to her throne and she would never have recovered from the scandal of a sexual affair. Any sure proof of the slurs on her chastity would have ruined her value on the international marriage market.

Furthermore, the Queen had no private life to speak of, constantly surrounded by her ladies, who guarded her chastity even when she slept. A clandestine sexual relationship would have been impossible to conceal as, according to the Queen herself, 'a thousand eyes see all I do'.

THE SIEVE PORTRAIT

Quentin Metsys II, c. 1583, oil on canvas, Pinacoteca Nazionale, Siena

Much of Elizabeth's public image was based on the metaphor of chastity, such as allusions to Diana, the maiden goddess who swore never to marry. Further motifs included the use of pearls – precious stones closely associated with the sea and with purity. As Governor of the Church, England's maiden queen served as a replacement for the Catholic Virgin of former times. Indeed, as her reign progressed, the Queen's unmarried state became an increasingly important symbol of her devotion to her kingdom. She also used it to control her male courtiers, positioning herself as the unobtainable lady of courtly love. In Elizabethan poetry, sonneteers such as William Shakespeare and Philip Sidney addressed themselves to just such a lady.

The 'Sieve Portraits' celebrate the Queen's discernment and chastity, while also depicting Elizabethan imperialism, and are directly related to her status as a 'Virgin Queen'. They were painted by various artists, from 1579 into the early 1580s, and depict Elizabeth carrying a sieve – a symbol of wisdom and purity from classical mythology.

In the Metsys version, the Queen wears a striking outfit of black and white, which together symbolise chastity and constancy. Her simple black gown acts as a foil to offset the delicacy of her exquisite white lace ruff, veil and cuffs, as well as her jewelled girdle, pearls and brooch.

A humble sieve is a piece of equipment used by artisans to sift that which is desirable and useful from that which is merely waste. Around the rim of the sieve, an inscription translates as: 'The good falls to the ground while

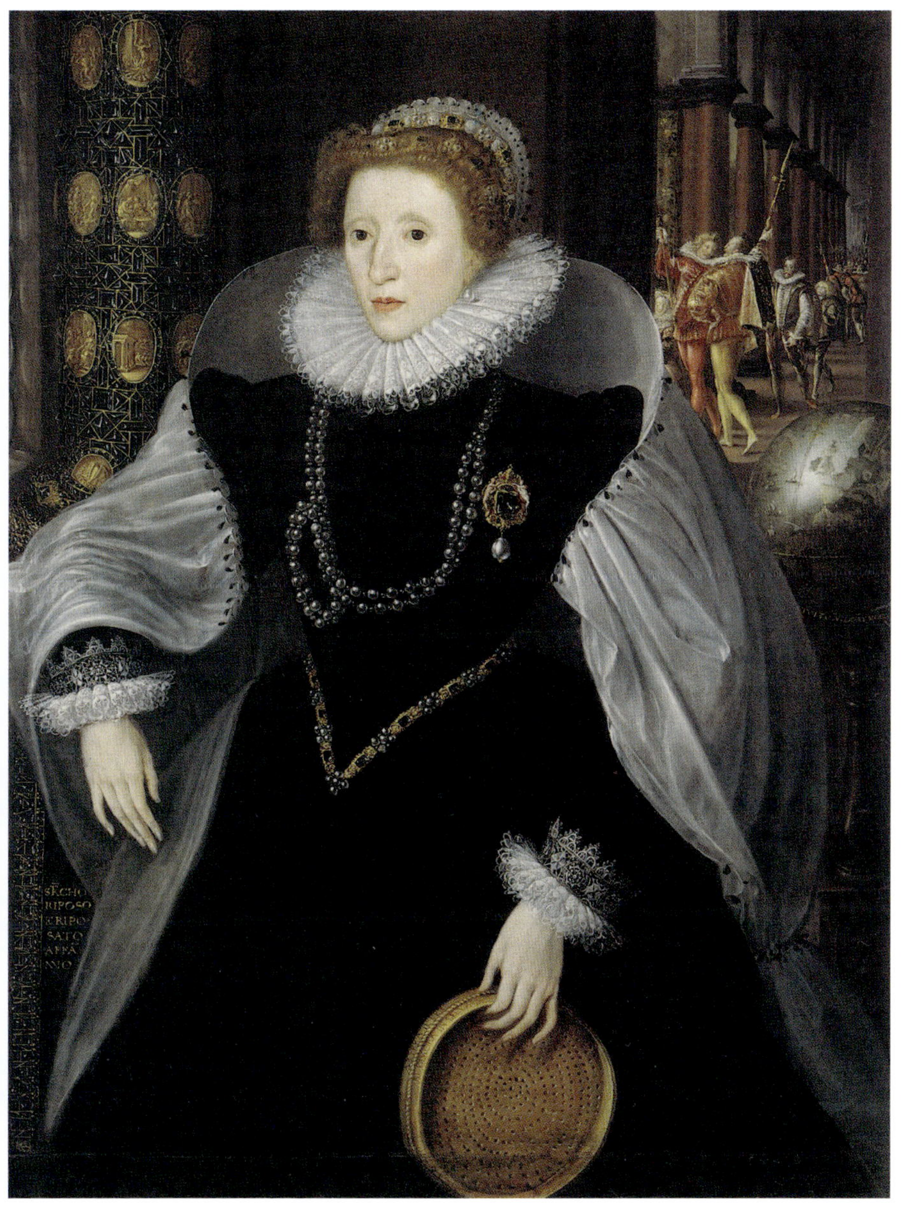

The Sieve Portraits are directly related to Elizabeth's discernment and chastity. Elizabeth is shown carrying a sieve, a symbol of wisdom and purity from classical mythology.

the bad remains …' This sieve is therefore telling us that Elizabeth is endowed with great discernment.

The theme of purity comes from ancient Rome and Vestal Virgins, who took vows of chastity and were not expected to marry. They served Vesta, goddess of hearth and home, and were tasked with the care for the sacred flame of the temple dedicated to her.

Petrarch's fourteenth-century poem *The Triumph of Chastity* relates the tale of one of these attendants. Tuccia proves her maidenhood by carrying water in a sieve from the River Tiber to the temple, without spilling a drop. The popularity of Petrarch's work made this story very familiar and Elizabeth would have read it in Italian. So, here she is presented as Tuccia and the sieve glorifies her virgin status, while associating England – and her imperial ambitions – with the Roman Empire.

Symbols of this new English Empire include a heavily embellished pillar and a globe, showing ships sailing west in search of the New World. This iconography would appear again in her portraiture of the 1580s and 1590s, most notably in the Armada Portrait of 1588.

The pillar reinforces the message of Elizabeth's independence and is studded with medallions telling the classical story of Dido, Queen of Carthage, and her doomed love affair with the Trojan prince Aeneas. On orders from the god Jupiter, Aeneas abandoned Dido and went on to command the Roman Empire. In other words, Aeneas resists the temptations of love for the good of the people. Importantly, the viewer is asked to see Elizabeth not as the female, Dido, but as the male, Aeneas, who rejects marriage for a greater destiny.

The globe behind Elizabeth's left shoulder is a statement of England's growing power as an imperial nation, engaged in trade and exploration by sea. The Queen's advisor and astrologer John Dee was the first to use the term 'empire' and he advocated the founding of English colonies in the New World. The presence of the globe here is a clear statement of defiance towards England's great rival, the Spanish Empire, and its colonisation of the Americas.

In the background, top right, we can see the courtier who almost certainly commissioned the work: Sir Christopher Hatton, England's Lord Chancellor. He can be identified by a symbol from his heraldic crest – the golden hind (a female deer) – which is painted here on his hanging sleeve. (Hatton was also a patron of Sir Francis Drake, who circumnavigated the world and named his famous galleon *The Golden Hind*.) The Chancellor, who is followed by a young page, is the only figure in the composition who looks directly at Elizabeth. Beyond him, we can see members of Elizabeth's Yeomen of the Guard, whom Hatton commanded. He had long been in great favour with the Queen and this work may express his jealous disapproval of her proposed marriage to François, Duke of Anjou, by emphasising her identity as a maiden. Nicholas Hilliard described Hatton as having 'a very low forehead' and not that handsome; it was his skill at dancing that first attracted the Queen.

Quentin Metsys the Younger (1543–89) was a Flemish painter, the grandson and namesake of the acclaimed Quentin Metsys (1466–1530), who is regarded as the founder of the Antwerp school of painting. It is known that Elizabeth I liked the work of the young Metsys because, as early as 1577, she tried to purchase his *Burial of Christ* triptych from the Carpenters' Guild in Antwerp. By 1581 he was living and working in London, confident of commissions and possibly having fled religious persecution. Seven years later he left for Frankfurt and died there not long after. Metsys is best known for this Sieve Portrait of Elizabeth and signed it (on the base of the globe) '1583. Q. MASSYS ANT' (for 'of Antwerp').

The painting was thought to be lost for many years but came to light in the nineteenth century, found rolled up in the attic of the Royal Palace of Siena. Today it hangs nearby in the Pinacoteca Nazionale.

5

NICHOLAS HILLIARD: THE QUEEN'S PAINTER

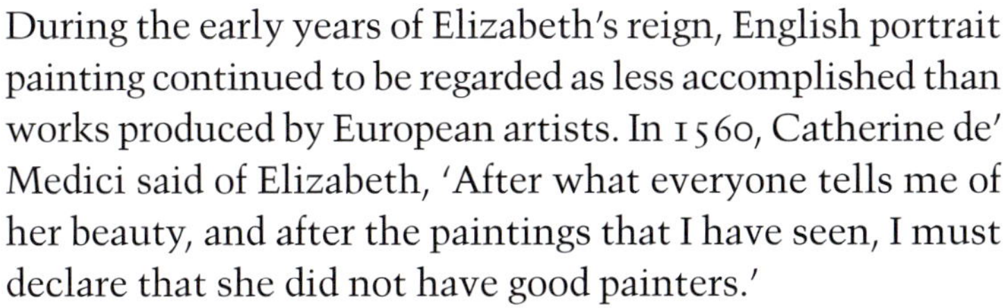

During the early years of Elizabeth's reign, English portrait painting continued to be regarded as less accomplished than works produced by European artists. In 1560, Catherine de' Medici said of Elizabeth, 'After what everyone tells me of her beauty, and after the paintings that I have seen, I must declare that she did not have good painters.'

However, there was one artistic field in which the English would surpass their European counterparts, primarily due to the mastery of Nicholas Hilliard, who considered the art of creating tiny likenesses to be 'a thing apart from all other painting or drawing'. It even went by a specific name. What we call 'miniature paint-ing' was known to the Elizabethans as 'limning'. Hilliard was the first native English artist to build a formidable reputation for his skill, not just in England but as far afield as Italy, France and the Habsburg Empire. As the courtier Sir John Harington noted, 'We have with us this day one that for limning is comparable with any of any other country.'

MINIATURE PAINTING IN ELIZABETHAN ENGLAND

The earliest known miniature painted in England is an image of Elizabeth's father, Henry VIII, painted by Lucas Horenbout around 1525. The technique and materials for producing these 'paintings in little' remained practically unchanged from the reign of Henry VIII to that of his daughter.

The term 'limnings' was borrowed from the decoration of manuscripts. These tiny paintings were produced in watercolour on fine animal hide, usually calf. The preferred vellum was 'abertive': skin that came from an unborn animal, as it was particularly smooth and had no hair follicles to hold the paint. The vellum was stretched and primed by being rubbed with an animal tooth – usually a dog's tooth – before being stuck to a support with starch paste. Playing cards provided an ideal backing for portrait miniatures because, generally, they were only printed on one side.

The vellum was prepared for painting prior to the arrival of the sitter with 'carnation': a flesh-coloured mix of pigments that covered the area where the face and neck were to be painted. Pigments were ground to a fine powder and mixed with water in a mussel or oyster shell, the ideal disposable container for small quantities of paint. Hilliard advised that the grinding of the pigments was to be carried out 'in a place where there is neither dust nor smoke'. If an opaque result was required, more pigment was added, mixed with gum Arabic or glair (egg white). The fine brushes (known as 'pencils') required to paint such minute detail were usually manufactured from squirrel or ermine hair. It was advised that artists should wear silk and not even breathe over their work for fear of damaging it with fibres or spittle.

A first sitting would last around two to four hours and the second four to six hours so, to pass the time, Hilliard recommended 'discreet talk or reading, quiet mirth and music'. A third and final sitting would finish the portrait. Commissioning a miniature portrait in sixteenth-century England was the domain of the elite and, in courtly Elizabethan fashion, each sitting would be carried out with discreet gentility and exquisite manners. Documentation exists to indicate that most sitters would have come to the artist's studio to be painted, with only the royal family and highest-ranking courtiers warranting a visit from the painter.

The completed portrait was intended to be held in the hand and admired. It could be embellished, by wealthy owners, to the point where the setting was more valuable than the painting. Jewels were not just valued for their monetary worth; they were also esteemed on a mystical and symbolic level. There was a belief that certain precious stones possessed spiritual qualities that would fend off evil, drive away fear and overcome sorrow. The size of these miniature portraits allowed them to be worn close to the body, thereby increasing their potency. Such was the skill in painting them that despite their small size they retained their impact. Ideally, they were to have all the qualities of fine art but on a diminutive scale.

Today, almost 200 miniatures attributed to Nicholas Hilliard survive, but there is no telling how many have been lost to us. It is frustrating to the art historian that documentation is sadly lacking and in most instances the painting itself is our only primary source.

A QUEEN'S PAINTER

Nicholas Hilliard was born in 1547, in Exeter, Devon, during the reign of Edward VI. The city was a thriving centre for one of the richest shires in England but also religiously divided. Nicholas's father, Richard, and his maternal grandfather were both staunch Protestants and successful goldsmiths. A signed, gold, seal-topped spoon and a silver gilt standing bowl by Hilliard's father are today in the collection of the Victoria & Albert Museum, London.

Goldsmiths enjoyed a higher status and earned more than artists, whose standing had not increased significantly since the reign of Henry VIII. Artists rarely left their mark on a painting, whereas goldsmiths, just like silversmiths, signed their work with distinctive designs, usually featuring their initials. In 1515, the Lord Mayor of London listed forty-eight livery companies of the City in order of economic and political power. In first position stood the company of mercers, or cloth dealers, the goldsmiths' company ranked in fifth place, while the painter-stainers held the twenty-eighth position. Paintings remained a low-cost item during the beginning of the Elizabethan period and Hilliard lamented that – due to patrons who refused to pay a decent price for a picture – painting was a profession that made 'poor men poorer'. However, during his lifetime the status of the artist would rise, partly due to the success of Nicholas Hilliard himself.

Collecting paintings was a largely alien concept to the average Elizabethan family but, owing to the connections of his father, the young Hilliard was brought up with an awareness of great art. Sir Gawen Carew, a member of Elizabeth's first Parliament, and his wife Mary were friends of Hilliard's father and both had been painted by Holbein. Mary's previous husband, Sir Henry Guildford, had been one of Holbein's most important patrons and his portrait can still be seen today in the Royal Collection.

The accession of the Catholic Queen Mary, in 1553, resulted in a Counter-Reformation in England and many Protestants, who wished to continue in their religion without fear of persecution, left to live on the continent, principally in Germany and Switzerland. Hilliard spent four and a half years abroad, in the household of the Protestant radical John Bodley, initially in Wesel – a German town around the size of Exeter with a strong tradition of painting. It had a marked effect on him, although he was not yet 10 years old. He later wrote that 'it breedeth or might breed more than a hundred painters for every one bred in England'.

After a year in Wesel, Hilliard moved with the Bodley family to Frankfurt, where he saw a drawing by Albrecht Dürer for the first time. He found this German artist to be an inspiration and later used Dürer as an example in his book *The Arte of Limning*. Written when Hilliard was in his early fifties, it combines an account of his life with a treatise on painting and is considered one of the most important documents in the history of English art.

In May 1557, the family travelled to Geneva, where Hilliard became proficient in French, a language that was to prove useful almost twenty years later when he was employed as painter to the Parisian court of François, Duke of Anjou. When Queen Mary died in

November 1558, Hilliard and the Bodley family returned to England, along with many other exiled Protestants.

A month or so after his son's return, Hilliard's father travelled to London as a representative of the Goldsmiths' guild and, while there, met Robert Brandon, one of the new Queen's royal goldsmiths. Hilliard Senior was able to secure a prestigious appointment for his son, as an apprentice to Brandon, beginning in November 1562, when Nicholas was 15. The master paid a fee to the Goldsmiths Company at the 'binding' of the apprentice, who was then fed, housed and clothed by his employer, as well as being taught English and Latin, during his indenture. In Europe, the period of 'binding' could be between ten and fourteen years, but in London it was usually seven.

Hilliard moved with Brandon and his family into premises in Cheapside, London. The area became known as 'Goldsmiths Row' because of the number of jewellers on its south side. As early as 1500, the Venetian ambassador, Andrea Trevisano, mentioned fifty-two goldsmiths' shops in a single street. Cheapside was one of the most prestigious areas in the city and at the centre of Elizabethan trade. After remaining in Brandon's service for almost seven years, Hilliard qualified and gained his 'freedom' from the Worshipful Company of Goldsmiths on 29 July 1569, at Goldsmiths Hall, London.

Between 1566 and 1568, there are records of sixty émigré goldsmiths applying to work in London, bringing with them superior skills in jewellery making. Hilliard's training with Brandon appears to have been focussed on plate, but he also worked alongside émigré craftsmen and, after finishing his indenture, he and his brother John were making and selling gold rings. It is likely that he came across miniature paintings during his training because the pictures were often enclosed in gold settings, but it is a complete mystery how, by 1571, Hilliard had managed to become such a talented painter of miniature portraits – indeed, so talented that he could enjoy patronage at the highest level, including the Queen herself.

Hilliard claims to have taught himself to limn by copying the works of Dürer but, given the exceptional quality of Hilliard's work, many art historians doubt that he had no formal training. Instead, it has been suggested that he learned the art from the female limner at the Tudor court, Levina Teerlinc, but there is no firm evidence that they ever met. A further suggestion is John Bettes the Elder (who had been instructed by Holbein) or Lucas de Heere from Ghent (who taught John de Critz, future Serjeant Painter to James I). Interestingly, de Heere is known to have owned a collection of drawings by Dürer, a rare possession in Elizabethan London. Fourteen miniatures by Hilliard are known to have been produced between 1571 and 1576 and even amongst these earliest examples, it is clear that he is unusually accomplished.

On 22 July 1571, a now lost miniature of Queen Elizabeth was sent to the French court. No other contemporary Englishman was capable of producing this portrait, described as being of very high quality. It was most likely painted by the young Hilliard, who only two years before had finished his apprenticeship as a goldsmith.

In *The Arte of Limning*, Hilliard looks back to 1571 when he was 24 and when 'first I came in her Highnes presence to draw'. Their meeting took place, most likely at the Queen's request, in 'the open ally of a goodly garden', where she found the light more flattering to her complexion. In summer, the court would usually leave on progress to travel the country, but the year of 1571 was spent around London. From July, Elizabeth was at Hampton Court Palace – her Privy Council is known to have met there on 10 July – and this is where the now lost portrait was probably painted.

Hilliard's earliest surviving miniature of the Queen dates to 1572 and is in the collection of the National Portrait Gallery in London. Intentionally or not, he painted it on a playing card with a queen on the reverse. The introduction to his royal patron had come through Robert Dudley, Earl of Leicester, and the link was Robert Brandon, Hilliard's former master, who had acted as a money lender and a banker for the Earl. Through this fortunate connection, Hilliard found the greatest possible patron in Elizabethan England, for Dudley was both the Queen's favourite and a serious art collector.

During the early years, Elizabeth and Dudley were the only sitters that Hilliard painted twice and in 1575 he painted miniatures of them measuring 18 x 15mm – smaller than usual and slightly oval, indicating the influence of Clouet at the French court. They are not a true pair because the couple face in the same direction, but the implied message is clear. Robert Dudley had ambitions to marry Elizabeth and this is the only known example of a courtier – albeit a privileged one – commissioning a portrait of himself to be displayed beside one of the Queen.

In July 1576, Hilliard married Robert Brandon's daughter Alice at the Church of St Vedast in London. Soon afterwards he accepted employment at the court of Catherine de' Medici's youngest son, François, Duke of Anjou, where Hilliard was described as 'Nicolas Leyliar, Peintre Anglois'. He was awarded the position of 'Valet de Garderobe' to the duke, on a salary of 600 livres, and travelled to France in the train of Elizabeth's ambassador, Sir Amias Paulet, a West Countryman like himself and a firm Protestant.

Marriage negotiations between Queen Elizabeth and Anjou prompted her to request his portrait from Hilliard. However, aware of her father's experience of marrying Anne of Cleves on the strength of a portrait by Holbein, she always claimed that she would never marry anyone without first seeing him in the flesh. And, in this instance, there was an additional precaution.

Anjou had contracted smallpox in childhood, which led to dramatic tales about his supposed deformities. A portrait of him had been sent to Elizabeth in 1572, by his mother, but it revealed no sign of disfigurement. The French ambassador asked for the Queen's opinion of the painting and – hinting at the problem – Dudley queried that perhaps the portrait did not look *exactly* like the duke? When pushed further, the Earl related that Elizabeth was hoping 'the accident with his face' would fade in time. The Queen was much more tactful and replied simply that the portrait had made her want to know more about her suitor's appearance and his disposition.

Hilliard spent much of his two years in Paris working as a goldsmith, aligned with the French goldsmiths' company, the *Orfèvrerie*. His miniature self-portrait of 1577, the only certain image of the artist and today in the collection of the V&A, shows an exceptionally well dressed and attractive man, brimming with confidence. Before leaving the French capital, in 1578, he painted the 18-year-old Francis Bacon. Both young men had arrived in Paris with Sir Amias Paulet two years previously, with Bacon acting as the ambassador's administrator.

Clearly, Hilliard had not made his fortune in France because he appears to have been short of funds in July 1579, when he borrowed £70 from Robert Brandon, using his parents' house in Exeter as collateral. Rather worryingly, should the loan not be repaid within a year, the family home was to be forfeited. Happily, Nicholas Hilliard paid just in time and their home was spared.

He then established a studio in Gutter Lane, London, and employed Isaac Oliver, most likely as a casual student rather than an indentured apprentice. The agreement was probably informal, meaning that Hilliard would not have to pay Oliver's board and lodging, nor the fees to the Goldsmiths Company. It is also unlikely the arrangement was for seven years. In engaging and training Oliver, Hilliard was no doubt unaware that he was helping to create his greatest rival.

Commissions were plentiful and Hilliard was painting 'in great' and 'in little', producing seals, designs for prints, decorative work and medals, but despite all this output, he never seems to have earned enough to satisfy his needs. He retained the patronage of Anjou and produced several portraits of Elizabeth and the Duke, but in 1584 Anjou died. Worse was to come when Dudley secretly married Lettice, Dowager Countess of Essex. Hilliard realised that his best patron might no longer be in favour with the Queen (although the estrangement turned out to be temporary) and he began casting around for new support. He had received no payments from the parsimonious Elizabeth for around two years and petitioned Dudley for help in the matter. The exact amount owed to Hilliard by the Crown is difficult to discern, but a subsequent plea to the Chancellor of the Exchequer resulted in Hilliard receiving the lease on Yelvertoft, a village in the Daventry district of Northamptonshire, which was valued at more than £23 a year.

During the 1580s, Hilliard's portraits of Elizabeth become noticeably less personal. Her last suitor had died, her greatest love was now married and Elizabeth withdrew from the royal marriage market. But demand for her portraits as diplomatic gifts, and for the walls of loyal subjects, grew, particularly in response to threats from Catholic Spain. Showing the Queen's portrait demonstrated patriotism and Protestant credentials. Hilliard also had commissions from fashionable patrons wishing to enhance their position at court by seeking him to paint them 'in little'.

In the mid-1580s, Hilliard was charging £3 for a miniature painting – a large sum to the average Elizabethan, when most people earned less than that a year. The Queen was often in his debt, but this seems unlikely to have been the primary reason for Hilliard's financial worries. He and Alice had a large family of children to feed and he enjoyed an extravagant lifestyle that included opulent clothes, enabling him to present himself as the equal of high-ranking courtiers such as Dudley. In 1585, he borrowed £50 from an orphan fund administered by his father-in-law, Robert Brandon.

When Robert Dudley died in 1588, following a brief illness, it was the end of an era for Hilliard. In addition, Isaac Oliver now began to emerge as a talented competitor. His first work was a miniature of 1587 signed 'I O' in imitation of the goldsmith's mark employed by Hilliard. This was followed in 1588 by several more accomplished works. Oval in form, with gold inscriptions informing the viewer of the year and age of the sitter, they clearly borrow from his teacher. Two years later, Oliver produced a self-portrait depicting a confident young man, hand on hip, gazing unflinchingly at the viewer. Hilliard's principal competitor had come of age.

In what must have been an enormous blow for Hilliard, the Queen chose Oliver to produce a new pattern of her face to be copied for miniatures. But the older artist's relief, on seeing the result, must have been palpable. With blunt and misguided realism, Oliver had painted the Queen with a wrinkled forehead, an auburn wig, sunken eyes and a long hooked nose. Oliver's pattern was almost certainly sketched from life in 1590/92. Produced in watercolour on vellum, it is now part of the V&A collection.

It was so unflattering that Elizabeth immediately returned to Hilliard who, in response to her horrified reaction, now created his comforting 'mask of youth'. Soft and flattering, it cast the Queen as an ageless beauty. This mask of youth also had its equivalent in poetry and literature, transforming the Virgin Queen into an icon, very much apart from ordinary women.

In 1596, the Privy Council decreed that no new portraits of Elizabeth were to be produced without the approval of her Serjeant Painter, George Gower. A native Englishman, Gower was a gentleman by birth whose work was very fashionable at the time. The task of censorship, set for him by the Queen, was not solely due to her vanity. It was believed that images of an ageing monarch, without an heir, would hint at instability and so henceforth those that did not conform were destroyed.

Queen Elizabeth I

Nicholas Hilliard, c. 1595–1600, watercolour on vellum laid on plain card, Royal Collection Trust

Here Elizabeth is 'Astraea', described by the Roman poet Virgil as a goddess whose qualities included eternal youth, virginity, justice, purity and innocence. In the sixteenth century, this allusion to the classics would have been much more readily understood than today. There are

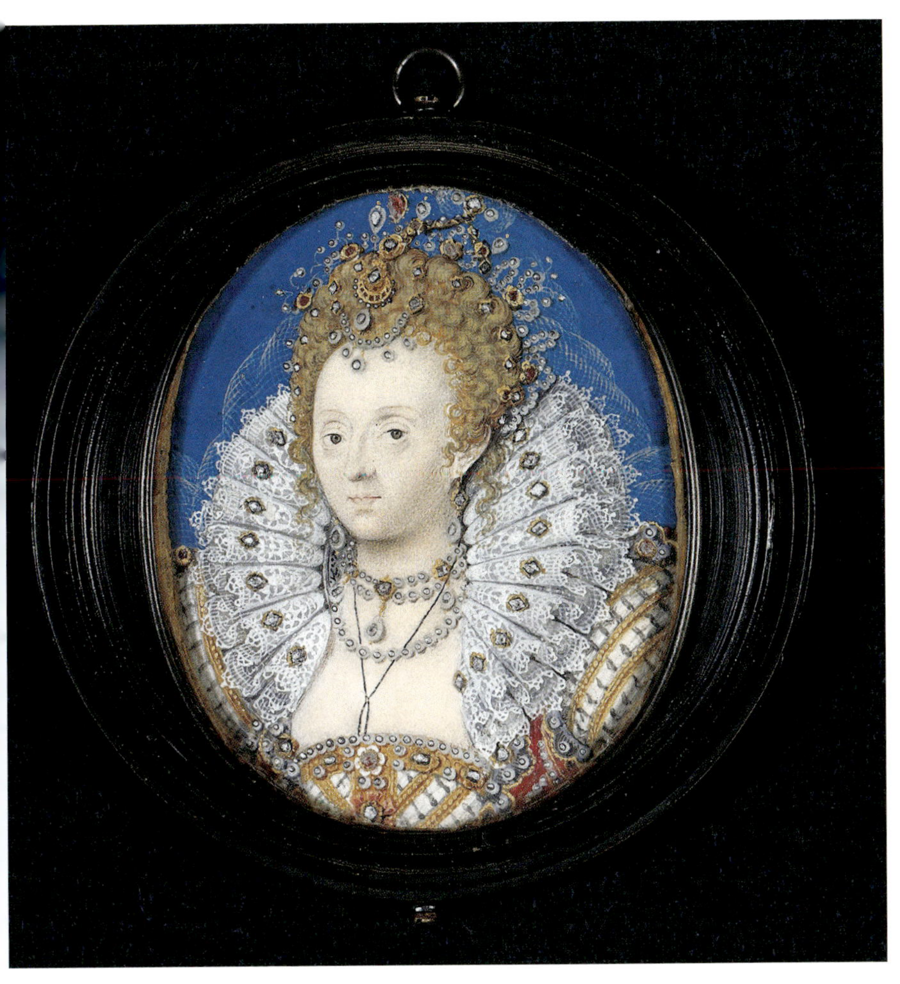

Nicholas Hilliard was portraitist to the Queen for thirty-two years. Most of the works left to us are miniatures, known as portraits 'in little'.

sixteen miniatures of this type by Hilliard, reinforcing the image of Elizabeth as the Virgin Queen.

It is painted in watercolour on vellum measuring just 5.4 x 4.5cm. In this small area, Hilliard has practically filled the frame with a magnificent lace collar produced by dripping a thick white pigment onto the vellum. The thickness of the dribbled paint (rather like the icing on a cake) means the ruff stands higher than the rest of the painting and, when viewed in directional light, it cleverly casts a shadow that imitates real lace.

The illusion of gold jewellery is created by applying an ochre-coloured ground that is then overlaid with finely ground gold powder, named 'shell gold' after the mussel or oyster shells in which it was mixed with gum or glue. For the numerous pearls, white pigment is overlaid with silver, creating a realistic sheen.

In these stylised portraits of the Queen, it is the magnificence of Elizabeth's dress and jewellery that become the primary focus. Their splendour is intended to represent the divine glory and majesty of monarchy, representing it as a body apart from the physical being of an ageing queen.

Hilliard was portraitist to the Queen for thirty-two years. She first sat for him in 1571 and he was still creating images of her until her death in 1603. Most of the works left to us are portraits 'in little', but Hilliard also painted her in oils 'in great'.

Queen Elizabeth I (The Pelican Portrait)

Nicholas Hilliard, c. 1573/75, oil on panel, Walker Art Gallery, Liverpool, and (The Phoenix Portrait) 1573/75, oil on panel, National Portrait Gallery, London (on display at Tate Britain since 1965)

The titles given to these paintings refer to the jewelled pendants at Elizabeth's breast, a phoenix in one and a pelican in the other. The phoenix is a mythological bird that never dies. It was believed to live for 500 years before being consumed by fire and then reborn. According to mythology, only one phoenix can live at any one time and so, for Elizabeth, this portrait represented the hereditary monarchy, her individuality, uniqueness and longevity. It was regarded as a symbol of the Resurrection and eternal life, offering the Elizabethan viewer reassurance that the Tudor dynasty would be regenerated. In reality, of course, there were no political plans in place for her successor.

The *Pelican Portrait* references the ancient belief that in times of hardship, a pelican would peck its chest and feed the blood to its hungry young. The pelican symbolises the sacrifice of Christ on the cross and implies that Elizabeth cares for the Church of England in the same fashion as Christ nurtured his Church. She is depicted as the loving mother of her people and protector of the English nation. A crowned rose to the top left of the picture represents the Tudor dynasty and, to the right, the *fleur de lys* confirms England's long-standing claim to the throne of France.

The sleeves of Elizabeth's dress are decorated with Tudor roses, produced by a method known as blackwork: embroidery in black thread on a white background creating lace-like patterns. Few examples survive today

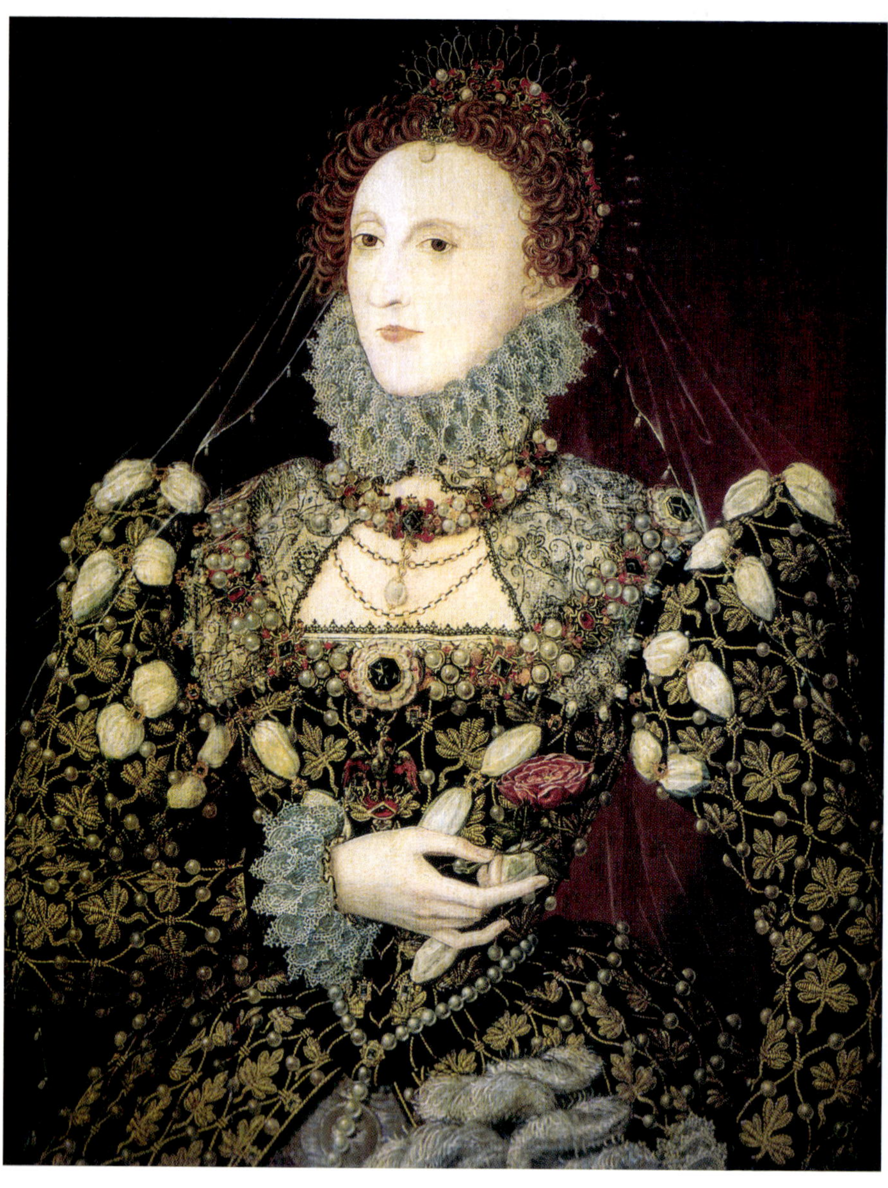

The Phoenix Portrait suggests Elizabeth's individuality, uniqueness and longevity, for, according to mythology, only one phoenix can live at any one time.

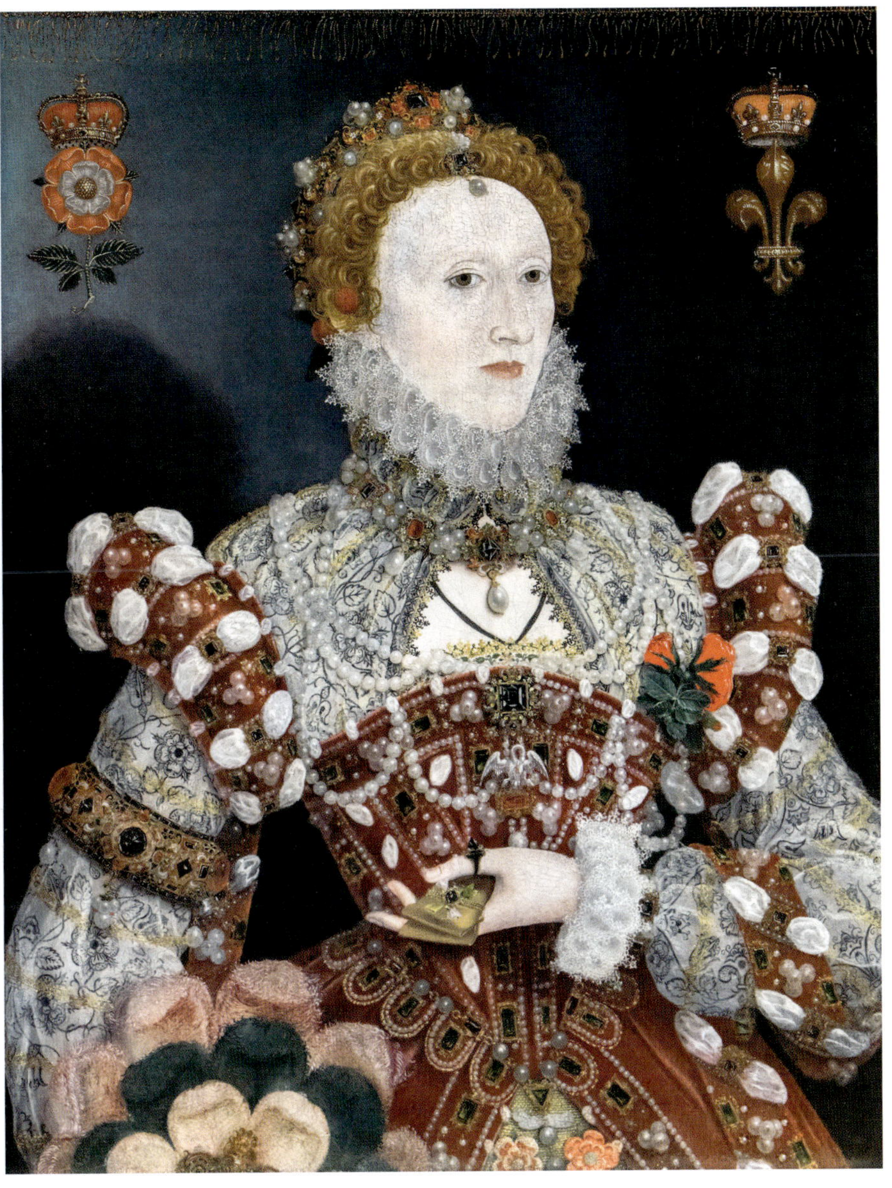

The Pelican Portrait references the ancient belief that the bird would feed its own blood to its hungry young, so it symbolises Elizabeth's selfless love.

because the iron oxide used in dyeing the thread was particularly corrosive and rotted the fabric, and so paintings such as this are valuable evidence of the skill of Tudor needlewomen.

The blue background in the *Pelican* panel is an underlayer, the original colour being a deep reddish purple, better complementing the red and white colours of Elizabeth's gown and headdress. The deep background has not been restored because opinion today leans towards conservation and not restoration – in other words, to acknowledge the painting's age and to aim to preserve what is left. In this case, that means preserving the original sixteenth-century underpainting of the background in preference to repainting it the deep purple colour most likely seen by the Elizabethan viewer. Conservation also aims to be reversable, recognising that techniques change and improve with time, so that in the future, conservation applied today can be undone and updated using more advanced techniques.

Attribution of these two portraits of Elizabeth I to Nicholas Hilliard is based on similarities with other Hilliard paintings, particularly a miniature of 1572, which seems to have been copied from the same face pattern of the Queen, produced when she was in her early forties.

Likely evidence of Hilliard's hand in the *Phoenix* and *Pelican* panels includes his typical linear painting technique, the distinctive brushwork, particularly in the painting of the hair, and the extremely fine and confident brushstrokes deployed in the depiction of the jewellery, for which Hilliard was justly renowned.

However, the ruffs and cuffs in each of the portraits have been completed using an obviously different technique. In the *Pelican Portrait*, we can see how delicately clear and crisp they are, painted as fastidiously as Hilliard would have painted them in a miniature. In the *Phoenix Portrait*, the brushwork is softer, with less detail, and less 'Hilliard'.

Although he refers in his treatise, *The Arte of Limning*, to the technique of painting in oil, there is little firm evidence that Hilliard did so himself. These panels are the work of more than one hand, and so the possibility should be acknowledged that they were produced to Hilliard's design and likely laid out by him, but completed in his studio by an artist more accomplished in oils.

Scientific examination has confirmed that both pictures came from the same studio and were painted in the same year, on Eastern Baltic oak panels that originated from the same two trees. Prior to painting, some of the wooden panels employed in both the *Pelican* and the *Phoenix* painting may even have been cut from a single piece of wood. X-rays have revealed woodworm in the boards and dendrochronology estimates that the boards came from trees felled between 1561 and 1593. As mentioned earlier, Eastern Baltic boards came from areas close to today's Poland and were imported into London because of their high quality.

Both paintings contain a green pigment identified as green verditer, an artificial and inexpensive copper carbonate manufactured in the sixteenth century by pouring copper nitrate onto calcium carbonate. It can be seen most clearly in the stem of the rose in the *Phoenix Portrait* and in the jewelled fan in the *Pelican*, further indicating that the two panels originated in a common workshop.

As mentioned earlier, Elizabeth's face in both panels is a larger, reversed version of a pattern used in Hilliard's miniature of 1572, and the line of the hands also appears to have been traced from the same design. They reveal a slight amendment to the fingers carried out at a later stage and, on close viewing, the alterations are today once again faintly visible due to the thinning of the paint.

The *Phoenix Portrait* has visible under-drawing. Infrared examination has highlighted drawing lines around the face and nose and, surprisingly, revealed two sets of eyes where the face was moved higher, possibly implying that the *Phoenix* panel was the first to be painted. These changes took place early in the painting process and are referred to as *pentimenti*, an Italian word meaning 'regrets'. The appearance of the second set of eyes is once again due to the thinning of the paint and it is a subject of discussion as to how visible the *pentimenti* should remain. On the one hand, these ghostly Elizabethan images are an intriguing and original component of the picture, while on the other, they can detract from appreciation of the portrait.

The *Phoenix Portrait* appears to have begun its life on the walls of the Deanery in Westminster Abbey, where Gabriel Goodman was Dean for more than forty years. In 1590 Goodman founded Christ's Hospital, Ruthin, in Denbighshire, with alms-houses for twelve people. It was in one of these alms-houses in 1839 that the picture was first recorded. In 1865, it was acquired by the National Portrait Gallery from Colnaghi – one of London's oldest and most celebrated galleries – and it has been on loan to Tate Britain since 1965.

The *Pelican Portrait* hung in the home of Sir Henry Knyvett in Charlton, Wiltshire. He was knighted by the Queen in 1574, the date this picture was probably begun. Knyvett was known for his quarrels and Elizabeth's Privy Council had ordered him to cease an argument with his neighbour, Richard Moody, over the ownership of land. However, their differences continued until 1580 when it was decided to settle matters with a duel.

Knyvett was gravely wounded and was forced to remain in the nearby house of Anthony Hungerford for almost a month. Elizabeth's concern for him is clear because the mistress of the house complained that 'the physicians and surgeons sent by the Queen had the whole house'. The portrait was passed down in the same family until 1930, when it was sold by Margaret Howard, Countess of Suffolk, via the auction house Spink & Son, to Alderman E. Peter Jones. In 1945, Jones donated it to the Walker Art Gallery, Liverpool.

If we accept the attribution of these two panels to Hilliard's studio, evidence from the *Pelican* and the *Phoenix* portraits reveals that the artist was working 'in large' in oil by 1573 and for a period around 1575 he was the primary portrait painter to Elizabeth, both 'in little' and 'in large'.

⸺◦∞◦⸺

By the 1580s, Hilliard was creating a different sort of miniature from those of the previous decade. The young gallants of the day did not want to be portrayed like their fathers; he depicted them enigmatically, with a focus on male beauty and sensitivity. There is an element of poetic sensuality in the sitters, who are mostly unknown. The largest collection of this work is today in the V&A, London, and includes *Young Man Among Roses*, c.1585–95. The lovelorn youth portrayed here, with his hand clasped to his heart, may possibly be Elizabeth's last favourite, the Earl of Essex.

The Victoria and Albert Museum in London houses an enigmatic image, dating to 1588/90. A young man in black reaches upwards to clasp a hand extending down through the clouds from heaven. It is not obvious if the hand is male or female, but inscribed in gold beside the sitter's head are the words *Attici amoris ergo* ('only through the love of Atticus' – or perhaps simply 'because of love'). Though the name may refer to Herodes Atticus, the second-century philosopher and Roman senator who claimed lineage from several mythical Greek kings, the exact meaning of the inscription is now obscure.

The Elizabethans were intrigued by signs and symbols; they could be employed as a pun on a name or perhaps to reference a recent event or family heraldry. The *impressa* was a device taken from Italian art and refers to a motto or a symbol of a private nature that could generally only be read by close friends. It was ideally suited to miniature paintings, which were by nature small and intimate. In *Young Man Among Roses*, the sitter wears black and white, colours associated with Elizabeth, and the roses are symbolic of her dynasty, signs that he wishes to declare his love for the Queen.

From around 1588, Hilliard used the innovative new concept of a free-standing picture showing the sitter full-length, which could also be displayed in a cabinet. A portrait of Lady Rich, for example, painted in 1589, is part of the Royal Collection at Windsor. It measures 57 x 46mm. The full-length court portrait has been reduced from life-size to the size and shape of a miniature, and this represents an important development in the history of miniature painting.

Hilliard's fortunes saw a downturn by 1589, when he once again owed money to the orphans' fund – this time £200. On another occasion, he would almost certainly have been sent to debtors' prison over an arrears of £20 had he not been rescued by a member of the Cecil family. In 1591, Robert Brandon, Hilliard's father-in-law and former master, died, as did John Bodley, with whom he had travelled the continent in his youth. Brandon left a £50 annuity to his daughter, but nothing to Hilliard. Three years later, Hilliard Senior died, leaving Nicholas the house in Exeter.

By July 1601, Hilliard was living, rent-free, with friends in the country, reduced to teaching drawing and the art of limning, for which his position of 'Queen's Limner' made him an attractive proposition. He also wrote his book *The Arte of Limning*, perhaps as a technical manual for his students.

By the end of Elizabeth's reign, Hilliard had retained his reputation as court painter. He provided the Queen with a comforting continuity of her image and he had responded to the next generation of courtiers who demanded something different in portrait miniatures. In 1600, he was commissioned by the Wardens of the Goldsmiths Company to paint 'a faire picture in greate of her Majestie', to hang in Goldsmiths Hall. It is not known if the work was ever completed, but part of the reason for its commissioning was typical of Hilliard: he owed the Company money, and the painting was to be taken partly in lieu of the debt. When Elizabeth died in 1603, he attended her funeral at Westminster Abbey and was awarded four yards of black cloth for his livery.

In his final years, he continued to produce his trademark oval miniatures, painting pretty women as well as men, and he began to experiment with light and shade – probably to keep abreast of younger rivals. Importantly, he continued to paint images of Elizabeth, whose popularity increased a few years after her death. It wasn't long before a disaffection with the new regime caused the English to look back with nostalgia to the days of 'Good Queen Bess'.

Hilliard was employed by the new monarch, King James I (who paid well and on time), but he continued to struggle financially. The death of his chief patron, Secretary of State Robert Cecil, was a huge financial loss and he never managed to achieve the same relationship with Jacobean courtiers as he had done in the previous reign.

With his bills mounting again, the ageing Hilliard was forced to give up the lease on his Gutter Lane premises. He pawned a miniature portrait of the King to repay a debt of £2 and it soon became clear that he no longer had powerful patrons to provide lucrative work. In 1617, Hilliard was sued in the Court of Common Pleas for the recovery of £40 (a considerable sum). His plea that the debt had never existed was thrown out of court and the septuagenarian artist was imprisoned in Ludgate, though released the following January. In August 1618, Frances Bacon, Lord Chancellor, whose portrait Hilliard had painted in Paris when the sitter was 18, came to his aid with a gift of £11 to 'old Hilliard'.

But his health was failing and, in January 1619, Hilliard was laid to rest at St Martin-in-the-Fields parish church, at the age of 72. His wife, Alice, and his greatest competitor, Isaac Oliver, had both died before him. He left legacies in his will to those close to him, including £10 to his servant Elizabeth Deacon, 'my attendant in this my sickness'. The money he left to Elizabeth was to be raised by the sale of his 'bedding and best household stuffe'.

Perhaps unsurprisingly – and in typical Hilliard fashion – there were no funds to pay the legacies to those mentioned in his will and one of England's greatest painters lies today in an unmarked grave in central London. A sad end to the goldsmith who, through his remarkable ability, became the first great English portraitist. His exquisite images of Elizabeth I and her courtiers came to define the Elizabethan elite throughout sixteenth-century Europe and for posterity.

6

SECRETS AND CODES: MARY, QUEEN OF SCOTS

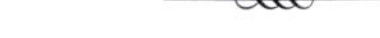

QUEEN ELIZABETH I (THE RAINBOW PORTRAIT)

Unknown artist, c. 1600, oil on canvas, Hatfield House, Hertfordshire

Painted during the last years of her reign, this portrait shows Elizabeth I at the age of 67. She is wearing an unusually low-cut dress and her long auburn hair is worn partly down and spreading around her shoulders in the style of a virgin. Her unlined and radiant face is the 'ageless mask of perpetual youth' that became her political persona as Gloriana. She is lit from the front, as was her preference, but the light appears to radiate from her in an almost mystical fashion.

Even though clearly an untruthful image, it is a fascinating one. The varied interplay of signs and symbols, combined with religious and political messages, have made the *Rainbow Portrait* the most perplexing picture of Elizabeth I ever painted. Art historians have proposed numerous and varied theories concerning its probable meaning, but its secrets have remained endlessly debated and tantalisingly elusive. It is possible that even its Elizabethan audience would have only been able to decode its message to a certain level, dictated by their own status and knowledge.

On Elizabeth's head is an elaborate headdress in which is balanced a crown. There is an illustration of a remarkably similar headdress in J.J. Boissard's book *Various Clothes of People of the World*, published in 1581 in Cologne, where it is described as that of a Thessalonian bride. This may indicate that the costume was to be worn at a masque or pageant. In this case, its meaning would most likely have been made clear to the Elizabethan audience by the character's context within the play.

Suspended from the crown is a moon-shaped brooch. It is the symbol of the moon goddess Cynthia, part queen, part woman, part goddess, and represents chastity and virginity. Large pearls are attached to the headdress. Round and luminous, they too are associated with the moon. Pearls were Elizabeth's jewel of preference and in this portrait they are numerous. The lengthy string of pearls worn around her neck reaches to below her waist and, for unexplained reasons, the lower pearls appear to be discoloured.

The bright, orange silk cloak is patterned with eyes and ears, perhaps suggesting Elizabeth is the watchful mother of her nation. Political intelligence conveyed sensitive

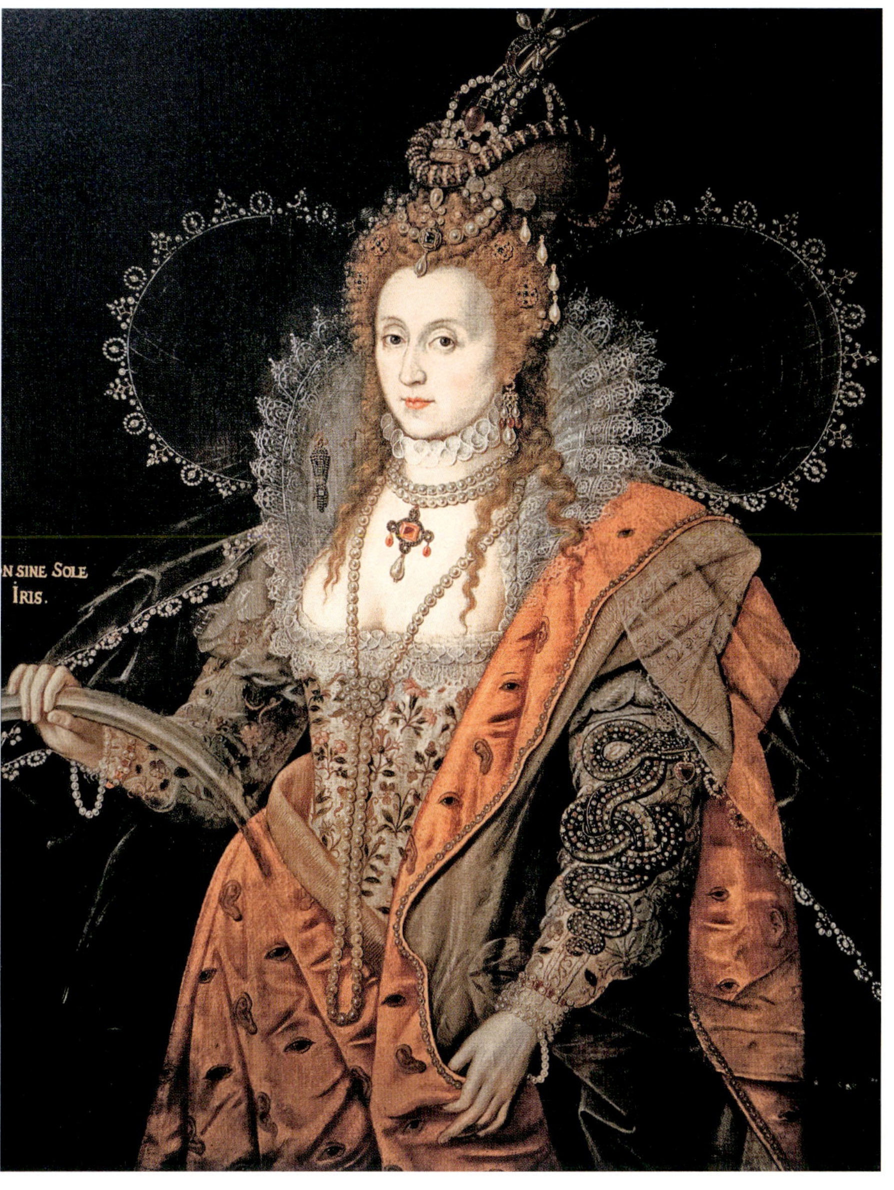

Painted in the last years of Elizabeth's reign, the secrets of the *Rainbow Portrait* have been endlessly debated but remain tantalisingly elusive.

information and Elizabeth relied on her advisors to be vigilant and to subvert the plans of her enemies through espionage and secrecy. Foreign intelligence was an indispensable part of Elizabethan government and essential to guard the Queen's life. Elizabeth nicknamed Robert Dudley, Earl of Leicester, her 'Eyes' and referred to her Lord Chancellor, Sir Christopher Hatton, as her 'Lids'. In the sixteenth century 'watching' meant 'guarding' and these pet names indicate their fierce protection of Elizabeth.

It is uncertain if the design of ears and eyes is on the exterior of the gown or on its lining, where they may allude to secret talks. Some art historians have alluded to unformed mouths in the folds of the cloth, relating perhaps to the Queen's motto, *Video et Taceo* (I see, but say nothing).

The most celebrated of the published dictionaries explaining symbols is Cesare Ripa's *Iconologia,* which appeared Rome in 1592. It was a book of emblems taken from Greek, Roman and Egyptian sources that personify allegorical figures and award them qualities and attributes that allowed them to be recognised.

According to Ripa, the character of *Ragione di Stato* wears a gown bearing images of eyes and ears, which represent political prudence. There was also a book of political philosophy called *Della Ragion di Stato,* written by an Italian Jesuit called Giovanni Botero, published in 1589 and widely disseminated. It debates the right of the sovereign to go against both natural and positive law if it is for the good of the state. Above all, the eyes and ears are likely to be testament to Elizabeth's political policies, which had succeeded for over forty years.

A snake decorates the left sleeve of her dress. The New Testament book of Matthew (10:16) states, 'Be wise as serpents and innocent as doves'. Serpents therefore represent wisdom and intelligence and, by the shedding of their skin, immortality. Emblematic of original sin, the serpent is on Elizabeth's left arm, where biblical images show Eve in relation to Adam. It holds a red jewel in its mouth that has been referred to as a heart, but could it be an apple? If so, it could allude to the fall of Eve and the fact that Elizabeth was guarded from such a fall by her purity and virginity. Or does the wise snake, holding a heart, represent Elizabeth's shrewd judgement, in following her head and not her heart? She certainly did this when it came to her romance with Robert Dudley. As could be said of most symbols in this tantalising portrait, the image of a serpent is acutely ambiguous.

Beside the snake's head is an astrolabe, a handheld model of the universe that represented immortality. It is one of the earliest symbols associated with Elizabeth. Her mother, Anne Boleyn, had drawn a sphere in her book of hours, *Le temps viendra* (The time will come), a book at present in the collection of Hever Castle. The most common interpretation of the sphere is to refer to the passing of time and the quality of constancy.

Painted on the portrait are the words, '*None sine sole iris*' (no rainbow without the sun), which is possibly a later addition. Ripa's *Iconologia* suggests that 'the sun is the symbol of light which in turn symbolises wisdom'. In other words, only the Queen's wisdom can ensure peace and prosperity. Catherine de' Medici, Queen of France, took the celestial rainbow as a symbol to express her hope of bringing peace to the kingdom of France. It represents the biblical covenant between God and Noah and, as such, could signal Elizabeth's ability to mediate between heaven and earth. A rainbow was once again employed as a message of hope during the Covid-19 world pandemic.

The rainbow Elizabeth grasps is colourless and almost unrecognisable. This has been explained by fading or changing pigments, but the colours in the rest of the painting have remained puzzlingly vibrant. The embroidery and fabric of the Queen's dress beneath the rainbow is clearly visible and not even partially obscured by residue pigment. Is this another symbol whose meaning has been lost to us? Perhaps it suggests that Elizabeth outshines all and her greater power has sapped even the vibrancy of the rainbow.

The collars of the dress are made from fine white fabric that is probably wired at the edges to float around the Queen like wings as she moved, and a gauntlet is attached to the lace collar to her right, which may allude to England's military endeavours and marshal strength.

The bodice of her gown is embroidered with English wild flowers that generally represent fertility and growth, as witnessed by the country during her reign: a secure Church of England was established, the Armada had been defeated, trade expansion provided wealth, country houses were built and the arts flourished. A gillyflower is associated with love and marriage, perhaps that of Elizabeth to her people. A pansy and a honeysuckle are interspersed with butterflies, deer, bears and even a man rowing a boat. A fragment of this dress is thought to have survived in the Bacton Altar Cloth and will be described in further detail in Chapter Seven.

The artist of this portrait is not conclusively known. The style of painting is Anglo-Netherlandish and the date *c.* 1600. A clear contender is Marcus Gheeraerts, although it is bolder than much of his existing work. Hatfield House archives reveal a bill paid by Robert Cecil in 1607 to John de Critz for 'altering of a picture of Queen Elizabeth', which may mean that de Critz also painted the original. However, the bright colours and the elaborate composition suggest the hand of the former miniaturist and competitor to Nicholas Hilliard, Isaac Oliver. Robert Cecil and Oliver knew one another and conducted business together; the Cecil family seat, Hatfield House, where the picture resides today, attributes the work to this artist.

If the painter is not known beyond doubt, then neither is the patron. The emblems discussed are those of secrecy and intelligence, so the men who spring immediately to mind are William Cecil and his son Robert, who controlled Elizabeth's Secret Service. Cecil died in 1598, so the patron is likely to be Robert but, with almost no documented evidence for the picture, all explanations remain conjectural.

The painting may have begun life at the Cecil home of Salisbury House in the Strand, London, where the Queen attended entertainments. The household moved in the 1690s and it is likely the picture was taken to the new Cecil seat of Hatfield House, where it remains today with all its secrets intact.

THE FIRST SECRET SERVICE

It is unsurprising that the *Rainbow Portrait* of Elizabeth I hangs at Hatfield House, the home of Robert Cecil. The mantle worn by the Queen represents a cloak of secrecy, whose eyes and ears protect her body and Protestant England. Father and son William and Robert Cecil used an intelligence network to hunt down Catholic threats and appointed Francis Walsingham to run the first state-backed secret service. Their 'eyes and ears' stretched inside the Catholic underground and all over Europe.

Walsingham was a Puritan with a deep loathing for Catholicism, Mary, Queen of Scots, and the agents of Philip of Spain. Elizabeth playfully called him her 'Moor', because of his black clothing, and his life's work was to protect her and to destroy the Scottish queen. His agents were called 'Watchers' and were the forerunners of today's MI5 (the domestic intelligence agency of the United Kingdom). The methods they used – intercepting correspondence, deciphering codes, double agents or 'moles' in the enemy camp and entrapment plots – are techniques that have continued to be deployed in the modern age.

Walsingham set up a kind of 'spy school' to provide training for recruits, such as academics who could decode messages. They usually arrived from Oxford or Cambridge, with an understanding of Latin, European languages and mathematics. Others were merchants, who were accustomed to travelling in Europe and could supply him with information from foreign countries. But Walsingham needed agents from all walks of life to infiltrate Catholic circles at home and abroad, in ports, market towns, suspect households and even prisons. The web of espionage included couriers, agent-handlers, seal-forgers, code-breakers, mathematicians, priest-hunters and interrogators. The end justified the means and the use of torture to extract information from prisoners was routine, while anyone found guilty of treason would be executed.

Information could be conveyed in invisible ink, such as the citric acid of lemon juice, which remains colourless until heated and then turns brown. A hidden message could appear on an otherwise innocent letter when the paper was warmed over a candle. Breaking codes was incredibly time-consuming work which involved looking at the frequency and sequence of letters. Sometimes letters were substituted with numbers, symbols or signs

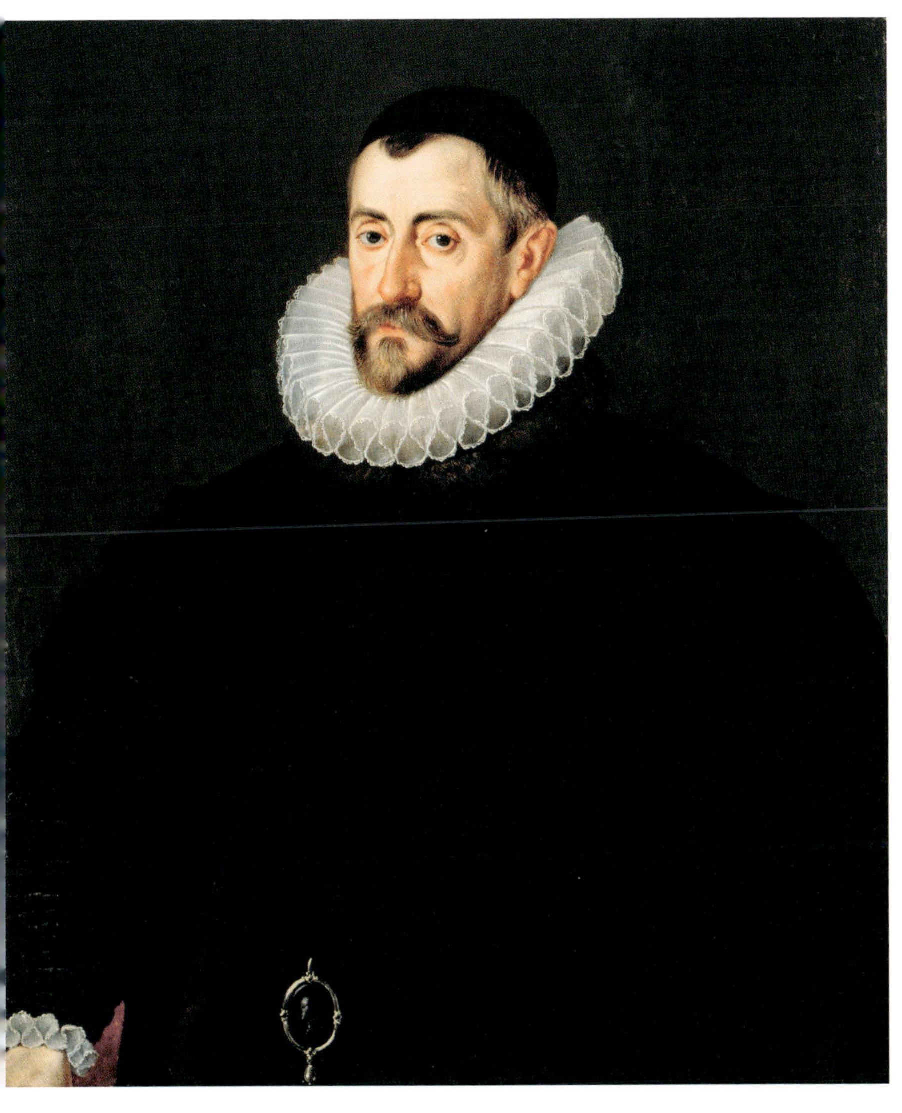

Sir Francis Walsingham ran the first state-backed secret service. The 'eyes and ears' of his spies reached inside the Catholic underground and all over Europe.

of the zodiac and only once the key was worked out could a message be understood. Cyphers were crucial during the 1586 Babington Plot, when Walsingham's agents decrypted letters to and from Mary, Queen of Scots. It would be this evidence that would finally prove to Elizabeth that Mary was conspiring to bring about her death. Queen Elizabeth failed to fund the network sufficiently so Walsingham was forced to spend his own money and he died in debt, just three years after Mary's execution. Elizabeth never properly rewarded him, yet he had done everything in his power to ensure her personal safety and to preserve his Protestant country.

The most serious conspiracy of the age came after the death of Elizabeth and was uncovered by Robert Cecil. The 1605 Gunpowder Plot would have been history's first major terrorist attack, when disaffected Catholics tried to rid themselves of King James I and Parliament – with three and a half tons of explosives. In Elizabeth's reign, a number of Catholic plots were uncovered, predicated on the hope of foreign assistance and all aimed at replacing her with her cousin and rival Mary Stuart.

THE RIVAL QUEEN

Elizabeth was jealous of any rival and she resented Mary, Queen of Scots, who was nine years younger, on a level that was both political and personal. On her first meeting with Melville, the Scottish envoy, she quizzed him about Mary's appearance. After asking if his queen was taller than she was, Elizabeth snapped, 'Then she is too high; for I myself am neither too high nor too low.'

As a great-granddaughter of Henry VII, Mary Stuart had a strong claim to the English throne and, unlike Elizabeth, she had never been declared illegitimate. She was the only surviving child of James V (nephew to Henry VIII) and his French wife, Mary of Guise.

Mary was the first queen regnant in the British Isles, although she spent her childhood in her mother's homeland. In contrast to the young Elizabeth, she grew up safe and secure – a favourite at the heart of the glamorous French court. It has been suggested that her cosseted upbringing did little to prepare her for the vicissitudes of her later life. She became Queen consort of France aged 18, but her young husband died and Mary returned to Scotland in 1561. She now faced the challenge of being a Catholic queen in a Protestant country. Having lived in France since the age of 5, she had little comprehension of the Scots, whose nobility was among the most rebellious in Europe. This – and two ill-judged marriages – would be her undoing.

Mary hoped to be recognised as heir to the English throne, which she considered hers by right. She wanted friendship with Elizabeth but she turned down her cousin's (surprising) request that she make Robert Dudley, Earl of Leicester, her second husband. To further the proposal, Elizabeth had elevated Dudley to the peerage, enhancing his status, and the match would have ensured Mary's loyalty to England. Instead, in 1565, Mary wed her kinsman, Lord Darnley. It was a marriage that quickly unravelled but it produced the child who would go on to become James VI of Scotland and I of England and prompted Elizabeth to say, 'The Queen of Scots is lighter of a bony son and I am but barren stock.'

In 1567 Darnley was murdered at Kirk o' Field, Edinburgh, in the Royal Mile, a few hundred yards from Holyrood Palace, where Mary and her baby son were staying. Within just a few months, Mary made a disastrous marriage to James Hepburn, Earl of Bothwell, who had been accused of her husband's killing. Elizabeth tried to warn her of the scandal, saying, 'I should ill fulfil the office of a faithful cousin or an affectionate friend if I did not ... tell you what all the world is thinking.'

Soon Mary was denounced by the Scottish lords and forced to abdicate in favour of her son. In 1568 she fled to England, where she hoped Elizabeth would offer protection and help her regain her throne. This was another miscalculation: her cousin *did* wish to preserve her life but the English refuge Mary sought became an imprisonment of nearly twenty years. Had she escaped to France, there can be little doubt that Mary would have remained free, but there was no assurance that Catherine de' Medici would launch an expedition on her behalf. Crossing into England was faster and she had assumed Elizabeth's support. Others thought so too. The English ambassador in Paris, Sir Henry Norris, told the French his Queen 'would not fail to favour and assist her (Mary) with what was needed'.

Many English Catholics supported the imprisoned Mary, especially in northern England, and conflict started quickly. These Catholic lords of the North rose up on Mary's behalf in 1569, although their rebellion was quickly suppressed. Within two years Roberto Ridolfi, an Italian banker living in London, was plotting Mary's escape and marriage to the Catholic Duke of Norfolk, with the aim of putting them on the English throne. The Ridolfi Plot involved Spanish intervention and its discovery by Elizabeth's agents brought Norfolk to the block.

In 1583 Francis Throckmorton, a Catholic acting as a go-between for Mary and Bernardino de Mendoza, the Spanish ambassador, confessed to a conspiracy to replace Elizabeth with the Queen of Scots. Londoners knelt in the streets to give thanks for the Queen's delivery and

Parliament passed the Bond of Association in 1584, calling on all Englishmen to take an oath to seek out and kill anyone plotting to murder Elizabeth.

In 1586 Anthony Babington, a former page to the captive Queen, was drawn into another plan to kill Elizabeth and free Mary. Cecil knew of the plot from the start and coded letters were intercepted by a double agent working for Walsingham. When enough evidence was amassed, the plotters were executed and Mary was put on trial. Elizabeth's councillors were able to persuade her that she would never be safe as long as her rival lived. She wrote to Mary, 'You have planned in divers ways and manners to take my life and to ruin my kingdom.' Elizabeth finally signed Mary's death warrant and then desperately tried to distance herself from all blame for the execution of an anointed queen. Mary Stuart was beheaded at Fotheringhay Castle in February 1587 and news was sent to the 21-year-old James VI at Stirling Castle that his mother was dead.

Once crowned King of England, James sent a velvet pall to cover his mother's grave in Peterborough Cathedral. In 1612 he had her body interred at Westminster Abbey, in a magnificent tomb with a marble effigy and a crowned Scottish lion at her feet. The queen who sought the English crown would have been satisfied with this final resting place near her cousin Elizabeth. The rivals fit rather neatly into the categories ascribed to them over the centuries. Elizabeth: strong, shrewd, cautious; Mary: charming, impulsive and a doomed romantic heroine. As female monarchs in a man's world, only Elizabeth ultimately survived but, in contrast to the childless Tudors 'of barren stock', every sovereign of Great Britain since 1603 has been directly descended from Mary, Queen of Scots. This is because the Hanoverian dynasty, who came to the British throne in 1714, were of the bloodline of Elizabeth Stuart, eldest daughter of James I and VI and granddaughter of Mary.

MARY, QUEEN OF SCOTS

After Nicholas Hilliard, inscribed 1578, oil on panel, National Portrait Gallery, London

Mary, Queen of Scots, is usually visualised as a figure in black, with a white headdress and crucifix. This is what she wore at Fotheringhay on the day of her execution, over a blood-red petticoat representing martyrdom. The famous image comes from the many pictures of the Queen, known as the Sheffield Portraits. Almost all are apocryphal commissions from the early seventeenth century, produced during the reign of her son James, after he acceded to the English throne. They take inspiration from a contemporary work by Hilliard, painted when Mary was at Sheffield House in 1578, and versions exist in the Scottish National Portrait Gallery and in the private collection at Hardwick Hall. They are part of what was a Jacobean campaign, undertaken by the King, to rehabilitate his mother's reputation, something he failed to do during her lifetime. This portrait in the British National Portrait Gallery, which was once in the Royal Collection, is probably contemporary. Recent analysis of the panel support has dated the wood to the mid-sixteenth century, indicating that it was made while the Queen was still alive.

The date 1578 marked the ten years that Mary had been held in captivity; the original was probably commissioned by one of her supporters and it is rich in Roman Catholic symbolism. A Latin inscription reminds us of Mary's

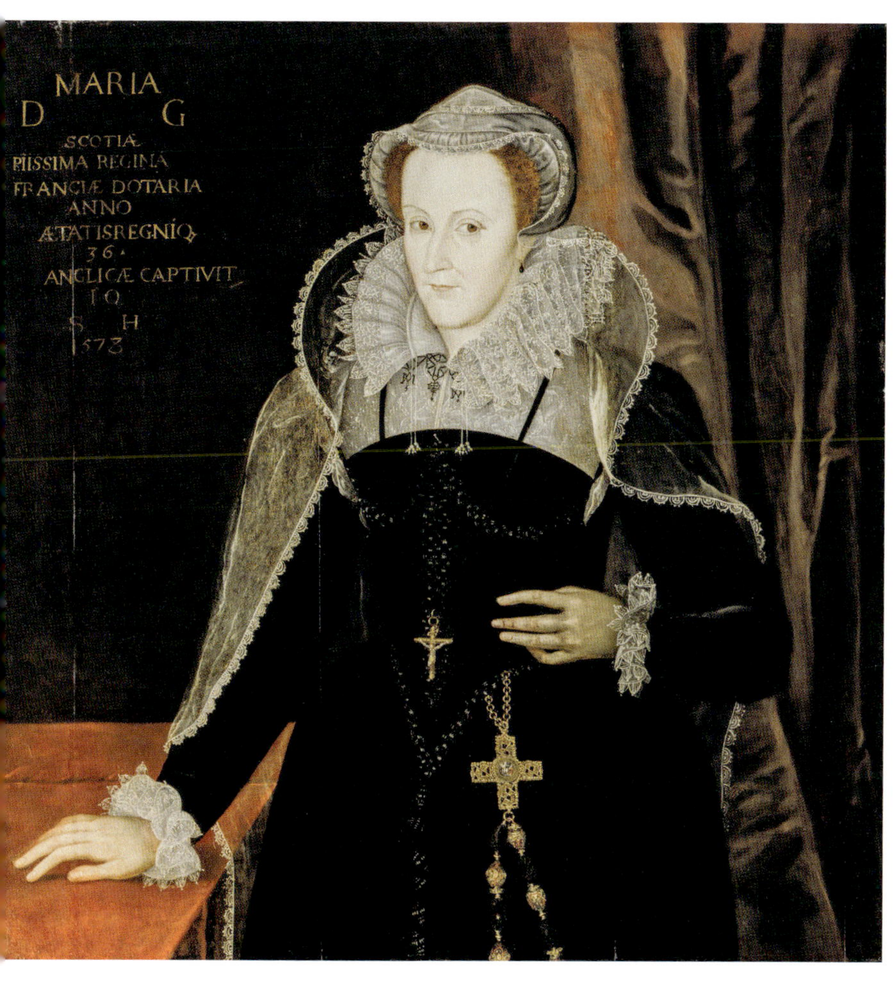

This famous image of Mary, Queen of Scots, is inspired by Hilliard's contemporary work, painted while she was a prisoner at Sheffield House in 1578.

lineage and the crucifixes, at her bosom and hanging from her girdle, reiterate her religious faith. Her hand rests on a table, draped with a vibrant crimson cloth – a powerful colour in the Church, representing suffering and the blood of Christ.

The simple black and white of her attire is striking, and worn together the colours symbolise chastity, a motif Elizabeth also used in her choice of dress. The black gown offsets the delicacy of Mary's wired veil and white lace ruff, while a black silk 'M' is embroidered at her neck of her fine chemise. Her clothing is rich, for the Queen was treated as befitted her high status by her custodian, the Earl of Shrewsbury, who spent great sums on his royal charge. Her rooms were hung with fine tapestries, she was waited on by a household of servants and she insisted on a cloth of state being mounted above her chair. It is clear that her imprisonment, all things considered, was a comparatively comfortable one, with Shrewsbury and his wife, Bess of Hardwick.

The cross attached to Mary's rosary bears the letter 'S' (for Stuart) on each of its arms. The other crucifix has an enamelled scene at its centre showing the biblical story of Susanna and the Elders. The tale goes that Susanna, a beautiful young wife, was secretly desired by two elders of her community. They hid in her garden and when she came out to bathe, they emerged and threatened that, unless she gave in to them, they would publicly accuse her of adultery. Susanna rejected their advances, she was charged and condemned to die, but at the last minute her innocence was established and she was saved. This image of a guiltless heroine is deployed here to proclaim that Mary is also the innocent victim of liars and plotters. The enamelled scene is surrounded by a Latin motto which translates as 'troubles on all sides' and reflects her stormy life.

Today, Mary's portraits do not convey an image of exceptional beauty but perhaps – like Elizabeth's mother, Anne Boleyn – her celebrated allure may have emanated from her charisma. One of Cecil's agents, Nicholas White, met her at Tutbury Castle and wrote to his master that she had 'an alluring grace, a pretty Scotch accent, and a searching wit clouded with mildness. Fame might move some to relieve her, and glory join with gain might stir others to adventure more for her sake.'

Mary's grandmother Antoinette de Bourbon, Duchess of Guise, described her as 'very pretty indeed', with an especially smooth complexion, red-gold hair and almond-shaped hazel eyes beneath a high forehead. She grew into an attractive young woman who was slim and exceptionally tall at 5 foot 11 inches. Contemporaries described her grace and lightness of movement and her hands, like Elizabeth's, were thought particularly fine.

While in France, Mary sat for François Clouet, a miniaturist and painter particularly known for his detailed portraits of the French ruling family. Clouet recorded, in fine drawings, Mary's transition from pretty child to Queen consort of France and finally to young widow. The latter, showing a 19-year-old Mary in white mourning – known simply as *'en deuil blanc'* – was widely copied. It is referenced in the Royal Collection as early as 1560, when Sir Nicholas Throckmorton, the English ambassador, remarked on Mary's intention of sending the portrait to her cousin Elizabeth.

By the time of the 'Sheffield' portrait Mary is 36 – middle-aged by sixteenth-century standards – with a thickening waist and the hint of a double chin. During her rule in Scotland, she had always been active and energetic, enjoying riding, hawking, playing real tennis, golf and dancing. Her long English imprisonment caused her weight to increase as her pastimes were limited to reading, writing and her great love, embroidery. It is likely that the curls of hair, visible under her lace cap, are artificial. We know that by the time of Mary's execution, at the age of 44, her red-gold hair was gone and those attending at Fotheringhay witnessed a macabre sight. When the executioner lifted her head and cried out, 'God save the Queen,' an auburn wig was left in his hand as her head, with short grey hair, toppled to the floor.

THE CATHOLIC THREAT

In the late sixteenth century, young Englishmen such as Edmund Campion, Robert Southwell and John Gerard returned to their native land under cover of darkness, crossing the Channel from France. They travelled in disguise and lived as outlaws. Just by landing in England they were committing treason, for which the agonising penalty was to be hanged, drawn and quartered. They were all Catholic priests who had been trained in Europe and then smuggled back home. They came to convert their countrymen back to the old faith and were prepared to die as martyrs for this cause. In his memoirs, John Gerard has left us a first-hand account of this cloak-and-dagger world and the covert activities of codes, false papers, aliases and disguises. Ironically, this was happening in the reign of Elizabeth, the most tolerant of all the Tudor monarchs, whose regime tortured and executed at least 130 priests.

The Queen's religious settlement had been a compromise because the England she inherited was not a Protestant country. Catholic and Protestant neighbours worked and traded together; there were Catholics at court and in the House of Lords. Many still adhered to the religion of statues, crucifixes and the Pope. The triumph of English Protestantism was not inevitable in 1558 and Elizabeth's attitude to her Catholic subjects was therefore moderate; she wanted peace and her emphasis was on outward conformity, rather than inward conviction. But problems arose as her reign progressed, forcing her to take a much harsher stance and making English Catholics 'Recusants': derived from the Latin *recusare*, meaning to refuse. Those refusing to attend the services of the Church of England were deemed to commit a statutory offence and could be fined.

The central question was: how could Elizabeth's Catholic subjects be loyal to the Queen and yet obey a papal authority that denounced her as a heretic and called for her removal? The famous *Regnans in Excelsis* bull, issued by Pius V in 1570, released her subjects from their allegiance, describing her as 'the pretended queen of England, the servant of wickedness'.

Then, on St Bartholomew's Day in August 1572, French Protestants were massacred by Catholics in Paris – an event witnessed by Sir Philip Sidney, Sir Walter Raleigh and Sir Francis Walsingham. Similar atrocities elsewhere in France resulted in thousands of deaths and caused panic in England with fears of a Catholic invasion.

The unwelcome presence of Mary, Queen of Scots, from 1568, presented a focal point for Catholic plots and Recusancy punishments were made increasingly harsh. In the end, the Spanish Armada was more successful than any amount of legislation in uniting the nation against the Catholic crusade. Anglicanism and Englishness were bound together and Recusants became potential fifth col-umnists, willing to join with foreigners against their own country. English priests were faced with an impossible choice: returning home openly meant immediate arrest, while arriving in secret appeared suspect. They resorted to safe houses and hiding places (priest holes) in wealthy Recusant households and behaved like the spies the government believed them to be. A number of these 'hides' have survived, with good examples in the National Trust properties of Coughton Court and Baddesley Clinton in Warwickshire.

It would not be until the close of the eighteenth century that the first Catholic Relief Acts were passed. By the 1830s, Catholics could worship freely and were no longer excluded from Parliament, universities and the professions. The timing was significant: it was exactly 300 years after King Henry VIII had broken from the Church of Rome.

7

ELIZABETHAN ARTS: THE GOLDEN AGE

The Golden Age of Elizabethan arts reached its height in the last decade or so of the Queen's reign, from the 1590s until her death in 1603, when the English Renaissance fully blossomed. Drama was the dominant art form, attracting an estimated 15,000 people from the growing population of London to attend the theatre each week. Christopher Marlowe was arguably the first great playwright of the era, but after his death in 1593, it was William Shakespeare who dominated the London theatre.

The Royal Shakespeare Company consider *The Taming of the Shrew* to be the dramatist's earliest play, believed to have been written before 1592. *Two Gentlemen of Verona*, *A Midsummer Night's Dream* and *Richard II* are examples from the mid-1590s. *Hamlet* was written around 1600 and *All's Well that Ends Well* is thought to span the period between the death of Elizabeth and the coronation of James I. *Macbeth* (also known as 'The Scottish Play') and *King Lear* are among a large body of work that falls within the Jacobean period.

GLORIANA AND THE ELIZABETHAN STAGE

In the early days of Elizabeth's rule, the morality plays of the medieval era were still being performed, as were stories enacted by strolling players. These were tales written in the vernacular, acted by semi-professional groups, generally in the streets, without scenery and with a minimum of props. But as Elizabeth's reign progressed, plays became more complex, playhouses opened and the stage of the later Tudor era became accessible to the public on a level that was only rivalled by the Church. Theatregoing became hugely popular with the poorer classes, who somehow found the time and money to go and see plays that today might be considered elitist.

The first purpose-built playhouse was the unimaginatively named Theatre, opened in Shoreditch in 1576, followed by the Curtain a year later. By 1587 the Rose, known for its connections with Christopher Marlowe, had been built beside the Thames in Southwark. In 1572, players were defined as vagabonds and criminals who were subject to arrest, whipping or branding. Religious and civic authorities condemned the playhouses as a scandal and an outrage. To avoid prosecution, theatres clustered around the Southwark area, which was known as a 'liberty'. In other words, it was outside the city boundaries, beyond the control of the Lord Mayor, and a part of London where all sorts of prohibited activities could take place openly. The original Globe Theatre opened in Southwark in 1599, to house a group of players known as the Lord Chamberlain's Men. They were a company of six actors who each took shares in the theatre to fund its construction. The young William Shakespeare was a member and wrote most of their plays. His genius for wordplay and dramatic dialogue was unprecedented.

The actors associated with these theatres were generally sponsored by noble patrons. Robert Dudley, Earl of Leicester, organised a public performance in the courtyard of the Bell Inn, Bishopsgate, London, in 1574. The Lord Chamberlain's Men had been formed in 1594 by Elizabeth's chamberlain, Henry Carey, Baron Hunsdon, and the Admiral's Men were under the patronage of Charles Howard, Earl of Nottingham, who in 1585 was appointed England's Lord High Admiral. Powerful patrons made an enormous difference to the opportunities available to the companies they sponsored.

Elizabethan theatres could hold as many as 3,000 spectators. They were built from wood and open to the elements, so if it rained, the actors and most of the audience got wet. Seating was available in a covered gallery for those able to pay the price and – for a lesser entrance fee – there was also an open section at the front of the stage, known as the yard, where the audience could stand. In 1599, a penny would gain admittance to the yard, a seat in the gallery cost 2*d* and a place with a better view and a cushion increased the price to 3*d*. Money was collected in a box, which was then stored in the box office. To put the prices into perspective, a quart of ale in a tavern was 4*d* and an hour with a prostitute would set one back 6*d*. In his *Plays Confuted in Five Actions* of 1582, Stephen

Gosson describes how 'it is the fashion of youths to go first into the gallery, then, like ravens where they spye the carion, thither they fly, and press as nere to the fairest as they can'.

There was little scenery in an Elizabethan play, which made descriptive words crucial, whereas costumes could help the audience recognise the social class of the characters. Women were forbidden to appear on stage and so boys took the female roles. It appears that at the age of around 18 the boys either transferred to playing male roles or left the company. However, this was not always true, because there is an anecdote concerning a performance that was delayed because 'the queen was shaving'.

Going to the theatre could also be hazardous. In 1587 a playgoer wrote to his father that he had seen a performance by the Admiral's Men in which an actor accidentally used a live musket. Tragically, shots were fired into the audience, where they 'killed a woman great with child forthwith and hit another man in the head full sore'. The Queen must have heard of it, for the Admiral's Men were banned from Christmas revels at court that year.

Elizabeth's reign was arguably the most splendid era of English literature, when names familiar to us today first found fame. Christopher Marlowe, the son of a Canterbury shoemaker, was Shakespeare's most noted predecessor and a writer who established blank verse as a standard for Elizabethan writing. His earliest known play, *Tamburlaine the Great,* is based on the life of Timur, a fourteenth-century conqueror of Central Asia whose ambitious quest for power took him from lowly shepherd boy to the throne of Persia. But Marlowe's most famous work is perhaps *The Tragicall History of Dr Faustus,* the tale of a doctor who attains knowledge and power by selling his soul to the devil. Marlowe himself was a self-confessed atheist and on 18 May 1593 the Privy Council issued an order for his arrest on charges of 'denying the deity of Jesus Christ'. Twelve days later, the playwright was stabbed to death at a lodging house in Deptford, possibly during an argument over an unpaid bill. However, his death has also been linked to espionage at the highest level: it's possible that Marlowe was part of Elizabeth's secret service.

A new genre of Elizabethan theatre was introduced by Thomas Kyd when he wrote *The Spanish Tragedy*, a revenge play and one of the most popular works of the era. A company of players under the patronage of Lord Strange performed it sixteen times in 1592. One of the characters is a personification of revenge, there are several murders and some elements, such as a vengeful ghost, are echoed later in Shakespeare's *Hamlet*. Few other plays are attributed to Kyd with any certainty. He was arrested and tortured in 1593 after letters discovered in lodgings he shared with Christopher Marlowe suggested that he, too, was an atheist. By December 1594, Kyd had died, aged 35, leaving little behind him to further illuminate the story of his life.

Ben Jonson's career was diverse; born in London, from a poor background, he worked as a bricklayer, fought in the Dutch war against Spain, became an actor and a poet and wrote numerous masques and plays, both comedy and tragedy. His bold and aggressive nature led him into serious trouble and he was accused of killing the actor Gabriel Spenser, only narrowly escaping the gallows. Jonson wrote numerous plays known as 'get- penny entertainments', which were quickly composed pieces written solely for financial gain. By contrast, he was also a man of letters who understood the classics, particularly Horace and Aristotle. Referring to his literary craftsmanship and

Jonson's views on the supremacy of classical models, the eighteenth-century poet Alexander Pope considered he had 'brought critical learning into vogue'.

A royal proclamation of 16 May 1559 forbade discussion of religion or politics in popular drama but it appears to have been largely ignored; during a theatrical performance at Cambridge University in 1564, Elizabeth was incensed by the sight of the Bishops Bonner and Gardiner eating a lamb and a dog bone in mockery of the sacrament. Edmund Bonner was known as 'bloody Bonner' for his persecution of Protestants during the reign of Mary I and, on becoming Queen, the young Elizabeth had shrunk away in horror when he had attempted to kiss her hand. Nevertheless, as a powerful show of displeasure towards this play, she walked out of the theatre and instructed the torchbearers to accompany her, leaving the performance in darkness.

Allegory and ambiguity were watchwords for Elizabethan poets and playwrights, as in the Wiltshire-born poet John Davies's poem 'To the Queene'. The poem appears to praise the Queen, but soon becomes more ambiguous. Davies writes, 'For you which downe from heaven are sent, such peace upon the earth to bring', a verse that could be understood as praise of the Queen, but which is also critical of Elizabeth's failing to deliver the mentioned peace at a time when England was almost continually in conflict with Spain.

In music too, Elizabeth was muse. A collection of madrigals by the leading composers of the day was assembled in 1601 by Thomas Morley, the most famous composer of secular music in England. It was titled, *The Triumphs of Oriana* and each madrigal finished with the phrase 'long live fair Oriana', an extravagant musical compliment to Queen Elizabeth I.

Members of the upper classes were expected to have an appreciation of music and because an understanding of it required intellect, it was considered a greater skill than playing an instrument. Music had long been associated with wantonness and unchaste behaviour and so Elizabeth would only conduct musical performances in her private rooms. She would surely have remembered that her mother Anne Boleyn was accused of an affair with the musician, Mark Smeaton. Sir James Melville, the Scottish ambassador, surprised Elizabeth while she was playing the virginals and he claims that she stopped playing the moment she saw him. 'She came forward, seeming to strike me with her hand, alleging she used not to play before men.'

Elizabeth and her court would spend a part of each summer on progress to visit and lodge with her noblemen. She was naturally at the centre of the lavish entertainments they prepared for her and was consistently addressed as muse, but careful judgement was required from her hosts. In 1575, the poet George Gascoyne designed entertainments for the Queen's visit to Robert Dudley at Kenilworth Castle in Warwickshire. In the opening scene of the play, *Diana and Zabeta*, Elizabeth was greeted by the 'Lady of the Lake' and hailed as the greatest British sovereign since King Arthur. However, when the character Triton posed the question of whether the Queen should marry, it was not well received and the play did not continue. Gascoigne claimed it was due to unseasonable weather, but more likely, Elizabeth objected to being associated with the lost nymph Zabeta whom Juno tried for sixteen years to win over to marriage but to whom she continually refused to yield.

The 1590s saw Elizabeth growing older and England still in conflict with Spain. It was a time of rising food prices, heavy taxation and social unrest, worsened by Elizabeth's refusal to name her successor. At the Christmas celebra-tions of 1600, the chronicler Anthony Rivers wrote that Elizabeth's make-up was in parts half an inch thick and he noted that 'she has become a *memento mori* of herself'. It is regrettably true that there was little precedent of older women in the arts, with aged women generally represent-ing sin, vice or even witchcraft.

The Queen's death could not be broached either directly or indirectly while she was living, but after she died in 1603, the image Elizabeth had constructed for herself became a stage prop. It continues to evolve today through artistic reimagining and reworking. During the forty-four years of her reign, Elizabeth was disguised beneath layers of make-up, wigs, elaborate costumes, jewels and masks. That raises the question of how much we can now truly know of the face behind the mask and of the real Queen Elizabeth I.

WILLIAM SHAKESPEARE (THE CHANDOS PORTRAIT)

Attributed to John Taylor, c. 1600/10, oil on canvas, National Portrait Gallery, London

'One man in his time plays many parts.'
William Shakespeare

This portrait of William Shakespeare is the only known image that has a claim to have been painted from life. George Vertue, a seventeenth-century antiquarian, notes that the picture was at one time owned by the poet and playwright William Davenant, Shakespeare's godson, who was born in 1606. Vertue adds that it was painted by 'one Taylor, a player and painter', possibly referring to

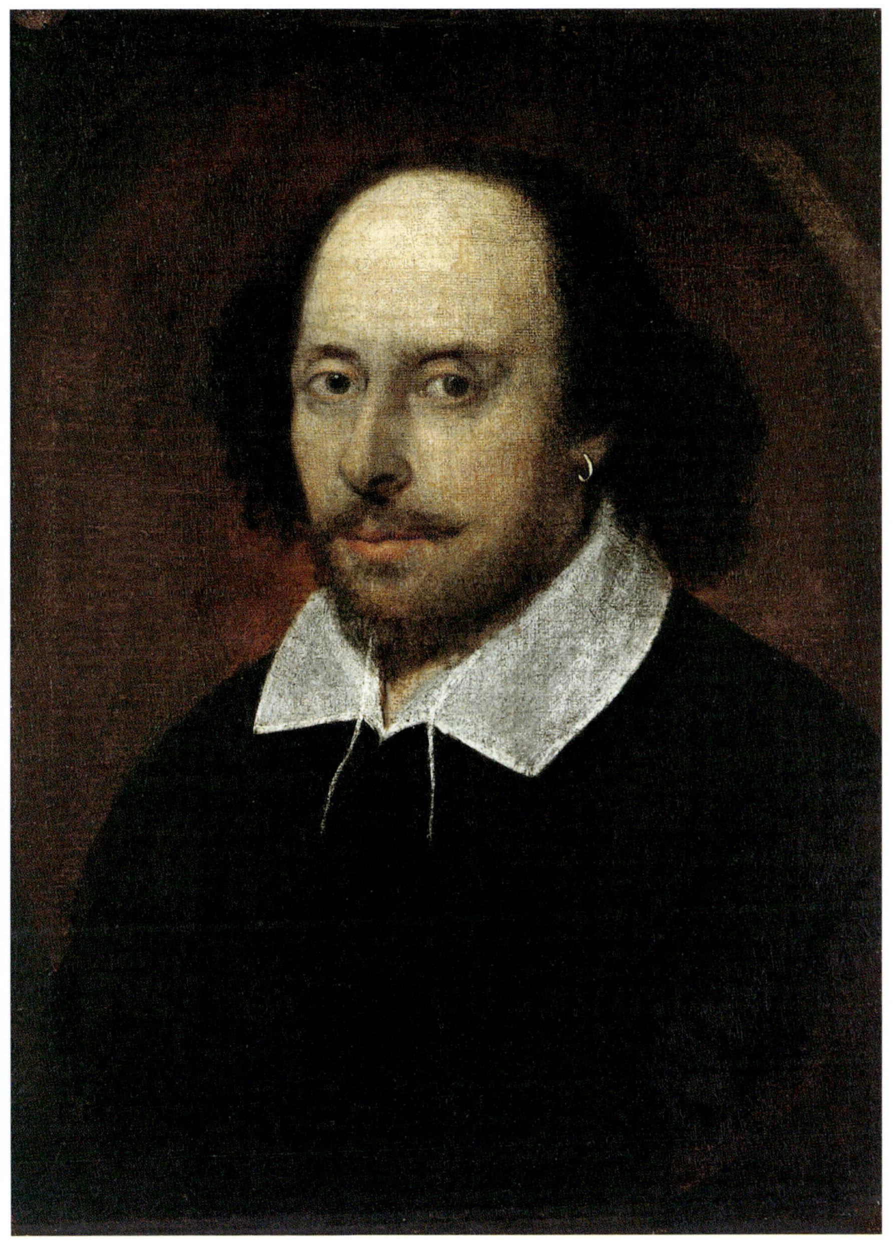

This painting of William Shakespeare, in the National Portrait Gallery, is the only known image that has a claim to have been painted from life.

the artist John Taylor, a member of the Painter-Stainers' Company and a contemporary of Shakespeare, but the name of Richard Burbage, artist and actor manager at the Globe Theatre, has also been considered.

It is named the *Chandos Portrait* after the Duke of Chandos, who acquired it in 1789, and it has been awarded the designation NPG1 because it was the first portrait received into the collection of the National Portrait Gallery, London, donated in 1856 by the Earls of Ellesmere.

Born in Stratford-upon-Avon in 1564, Shakespeare was the son of a glover and wool trader. His father made a name for himself in the civic life of Stratford, becoming Bailiff (mayor) of the town of around 1,000 residents when William was aged 4. The young Shakespeare attended the King's New School, the local free grammar school in Stratford-upon-Avon, where he received an intensive and excellent education, based upon Latin classical authors.

In 1582, aged 18, he married Anne Hathaway, who was eight years his elder and pregnant at the time. They had three children together, the lastborn being twins who were baptised in Stratford in 1585.

The playwright made his reputation by 1592, but the seven years between the christening of his twins and his arrival on the London scene are often referred to as 'The Lost Years' because practically nothing is known about his whereabouts. Shakespeare's name appears again in 1593 with the publication of his first long poem, *Venus and Adonis*, followed by *The Rape of Lucrece* the following year.

Writing for the Chamberlain's Men, Shakespeare produced an average of two plays a year for almost twenty years. Sadly, no original manuscripts of his estimated thirty-eight plays or 154 sonnets survive. The 'First Folio' is the first collected edition of Shakespeare plays, published in 1623, seven years after the writer's death. Five copies of these large and valuable books are conserved in the British Library in London. Before 1642, twenty-one plays were printed in quarto (named after the size of the paper on which they were printed). The earliest copies were anonymous and Shakespeare's name does not appear on a title page until 1598 with *Love's Labour's Lost*. Queen Elizabeth saw several of the plays performed and appears to have enjoyed them, with *The Merry Wives of Windsor* being a particular favourite. Since the eighteenth century, it has been rumoured that it was written after she commanded Shakespeare to write a play showing the character Falstaff falling in love. This is now considered unlikely, although it is recorded that Elizabeth watched the play. Her love of theatre made it respectable and the quality of Shakespeare's work ensured the Globe was packed with spectators every night. As he received a share of the box office, it made him financially successful and, by 1597, he was able to buy New Place, the second largest house in Stratford-upon-Avon. The writer then appears to have divided his time between London and Stratford, an exhausting and dangerous commute of around two or three days.

During the 400-plus years since it was painted, this portrait has suffered physically. The surface has thinned, parts of the face have been overpainted in a darker pink and the varnish has discoloured. The collar on the costume has been darkened by brown varnish and the erosion of the paint has meant areas of the grey underpainting are also visible, along with the weave of the canvas. On the collar of the costume, only minor areas of original white pigment remain unaffected. A small patch of test cleaning on the forehead reveals that, originally, Shakespeare was painted with a much paler complexion.

The striking gold earring stands out brightly despite the damage. It was painted with a lead tin yellow, a pigment common from the fifteenth to seventeenth century, which confirms it is an original feature. Earrings were worn extensively by men in the Elizabethan age to display wealth and status and ranged from the common gold hoop to extravagant elaborations of pearls and jewels.

Intriguingly, Shakespeare's hair has been substantially lengthened in a prior restoration and his beard is longer and more pointed. Ongoing investigations will reveal further information and assess the possibility of removing the old varnish to reveal the portrait in its original form. However, the paint was thinly applied and the surface abraded by crude attempts to clean it in the seventeenth and eighteenth century, and so it is a delicate task to remove the overpainted hair and beard without damaging the picture surface. It could also be argued that as the amendments to the picture most likely took place over 300 years ago, the overpainting itself is of historical interest and should therefore remain.

The ruff had fallen out of favour by 1610 and the simple black doublet and white open-necked shirt with loose ties were emblematic of poets and writers. They are also seen in the portrait of the writer Ben Jonson, Shakespeare's contemporary, and that of the poet John Donne, both pictures forming part of the National Portrait Gallery collection.

Following Shakespeare's death on 23 April 1616, two images of the playwright were produced. The Stratford Memorial bust was erected in Holy Trinity Church, Stratford-upon-Avon, between his death in 1616 and 1623, and an engraving by Martin Droeshout, an English artist of Flemish descent, was published in 1623, along with the first folio of Shakespeare's plays. The sculpted bust was installed in the church during the lifetime of

Shakespeare's two daughters and it was seen by members of the town who had known him. Ben Jonson is thought to have said that it was 'true to life'. The Chandos portrait bears a striking resemblance to both works and so it can confidently be assumed a true likeness of this remarkable English writer, described on his monument as a 'Socrates in mind and a Virgil in art'.

SIR PHILIP SIDNEY

Unknown artist, c. 1576, oil on panel, National Portrait Gallery, London

> 'Biting my truant pen, beating myself for spite, "Fool,"
> said my Muse to me; "look in thy heart and write."'
> Sir Philip Sidney

Sir Philip Sidney is the epitome of an Elizabethan gentleman – a poet, a statesman and a soldier. Born in Penshurst, Kent, in 1554, he came from an influential family that included his uncle Robert Dudley, Earl of Leicester. He was the grandson of John Dudley, Duke of Northumberland, and heir presumptive to the Earldoms of Leicester and Warwick.

His mother, Mary Dudley, was lady-in-waiting to the Queen and cared for Elizabeth after she contracted smallpox. The young Philip and his mother were both infected with the disease and Mary was left heavily disfigured. The poet Ben Jonson wrote that when she appeared in public, she always wore a mask, and four of Sidney's *Certain Sonnets* (8–11), first printed in 1598, are concerned with the face of a beautiful woman disfigured by disease. Philip was also scarred but no hint of this appears in his portrait.

The young Philip was sent away to school at 10 years old, to be educated at Shrewsbury School, Shropshire, before continuing his education at Christ Church, Oxford University. His stay there was cut short by an outbreak of plague in 1571 and he travelled in Europe. It was in Venice, in February 1574, that Sidney sat for a (now lost) portrait by the artist Paolo Veronese.

Home in England in 1575, he met Penelope Devereux, the inspiration behind his famous sonnet sequence of the 1580s, *Astrophil and Stella.* There was mention of marriage, but her father, Walter Devereux, Earl of Essex, died in 1576, ending negotiations. *Astrophil and Stella* is a sequence of 108 sonnets and eleven songs, which tell the story of Astrophil, his name meaning 'star-lover' in Greek, and his hopeless passion for Stella, the Latin word for 'star'. Sidney adapted the Petrarchan sonnet to write it and produced the first ever sonnet sequence in English. It ends when Stella confesses that although she loves Astrophil, she is unable to consummate the affair.

Sidney did not forget Penelope and they appear to have met again at court around the time of her marriage to Lord Robert Rich in 1581. There is no proof they had an affair, but he expresses his feelings for her in poetic form and there are puns suggesting that Stella is based on Penelope, Lady Rich. In Sonnet 35, for example, Astrophil says 'long needie Fame / Doth even grow rich, meaning my Stellas name'. If Penelope was Stella, then perhaps Astrophil is Sidney, who regrets his neglect of her when she became the wife of Lord Robert Rich.

However, in 1583, at the age of 29, Sidney married Frances, the 16-year-old daughter of Sir Francis Walsingham, in whose house he had lodged a decade earlier, during the St Bartholomew Day Massacres in Paris.

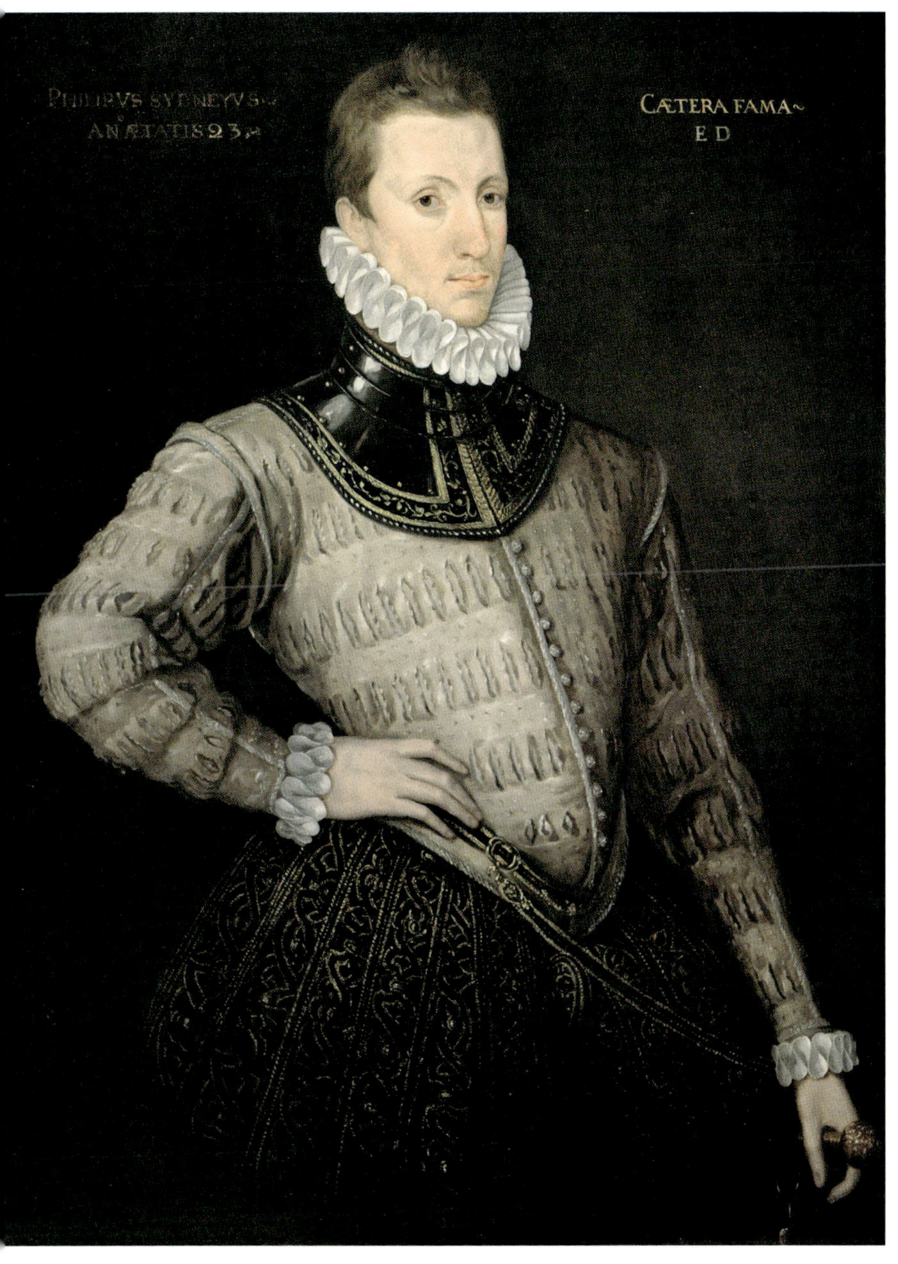

Sir Philip Sidney was considered the epitome of an Elizabethan gentleman – a poet, a statesman and a soldier. He died in battle aged 31.

The same year, he wrote the essay *The Defence of Poetry*. It argues that by combining the historical and the philosophical, poetry becomes more powerful than either individual subject. It is one of the most important tracts on poetry written during the Elizabethan era and one that can today claim the status of a classic text.

Sidney's two versions of *Arcadia* are arguably his most ambitious works. They were written with the advice and support of his sister Mary, Countess of Pembroke. Excepting the Queen, Mary Sidney was one of the greatest female writers and patrons in Elizabethan England and the person to whom Sidney dedicated the work. She also acted as his literary executor following his death. In *The Countess of Pembroke's Arcadia*, 1580, Philip Sidney was the first to put into print the phrase 'my better half' to mean spouse.

A few years after his marriage, Sidney travelled to the Netherlands to serve under his uncle, the Earl of Leicester. During the conflict with the Spanish at Zutphen, he was shot and his leg shattered above the knee. According to a famous legend, while lying wounded he gave his water to another injured soldier, saying, 'Thy necessity is yet greater than mine.' The bullet was too deep to be removed, amputation does not seem to have been considered and Sidney died a few weeks later of gangrene.

His body was taken back to London to be buried in St Paul's Cathedral in February 1587. The Lord Mayor marched in his solemn funeral procession, with a huge retinue. Although paid for by his father-in-law, Walsingham, it had all the appearance of a state funeral. Such an event, for a private individual, was not seen again until that of Sir Winston Churchill in 1965. There is a theory it was deliberately grand to draw attention away from the execution of Mary, Queen of Scots, that same month. Sidney was just 31 at his death and described as 'the flower of England'.

This portrait depicts him in his early twenties, wearing a piece of armour for the neck known as a gorget, under a white ruff, over an elegant white-slashed doublet. He is painted as a courtier, rather than as a poet, wearing expensive, elaborate clothes. The decorated sword beside his hip sends a message of his importance and elite status. There are numerous small areas of restoration in the face, which possibly indicated a small moustache at the corners of the mouth.

Composed of three panels, this picture is unusually made from two vertical panels of East Baltic oak and one of English board. Dendrochronology reveals that the picture could not have been painted before 1561 and was most likely from a tree felled between 1561 and 1577, agreeing with the attributed date of 1576. Apart from the old varnish residue, there are black deposits which could be soot, a very human touch perhaps indicating the smoky interiors of Elizabethan homes. The inscriptions may not have been applied at the same time and it is possible that they are a later addition.

ELIZABETHAN EMBROIDERY

Not only poetry and drama flourished in the latter part of Elizabeth I's reign; the Golden Age also extended to craft and design. The Queen's spectacularly embroidered gowns are meticulously depicted within her portraits and provide a detailed and lasting testament to the skill of Elizabethan needleworkers.

BACTON ALTAR CLOTH

Sixteenth-century fabric, on loan to Historic Royal Palaces, Hampton Court Palace

In 2016, an embroidered altar cloth in the small church of St Faith's in Bacton, Herefordshire, could be seen framed and displayed on the north wall, as it had been since 1909. It was clearly very old, but over the years no-one had discovered just how unusual it was. At one time, the vicar had apparently slept with it under his bed because there was nowhere else to keep it.

The embroidery is unique because it is the only surviving provenanced piece of material from any of Elizabeth I's extensive and impressive wardrobe of more than 1,900 dresses. She is wearing the dress that this particular piece of material almost certainly came from in the *Rainbow Portrait* (fig. 13).

The fabric has traditionally been associated with Blanche Parry, Elizabeth's Chief Gentlewoman of the Bedchamber. Parry was born in Newcourt, near Bacton. There is a memorial to her within the church and her ancestors lie in the graveyard. However, when she died in 1590, at the age of 82, she was buried in St Margaret's Church, Westminster, leaving her memorial at Bacton empty.

Tracy Borman, Chief Curator at Historic Royal Palaces, visited Blanche Parry's tomb while researching her book, *Elizabeth's Women*, and saw the cloth hanging on the wall as she was leaving the church. She suspected something special and alerted Eleri Lynn, a curator of textiles for HRP. The evident pattern cutting made it clear that it had come from a dress, and the high-quality silver silk, embroidered with gold and silver, denoted it belonged to someone of the highest rank. Its association with

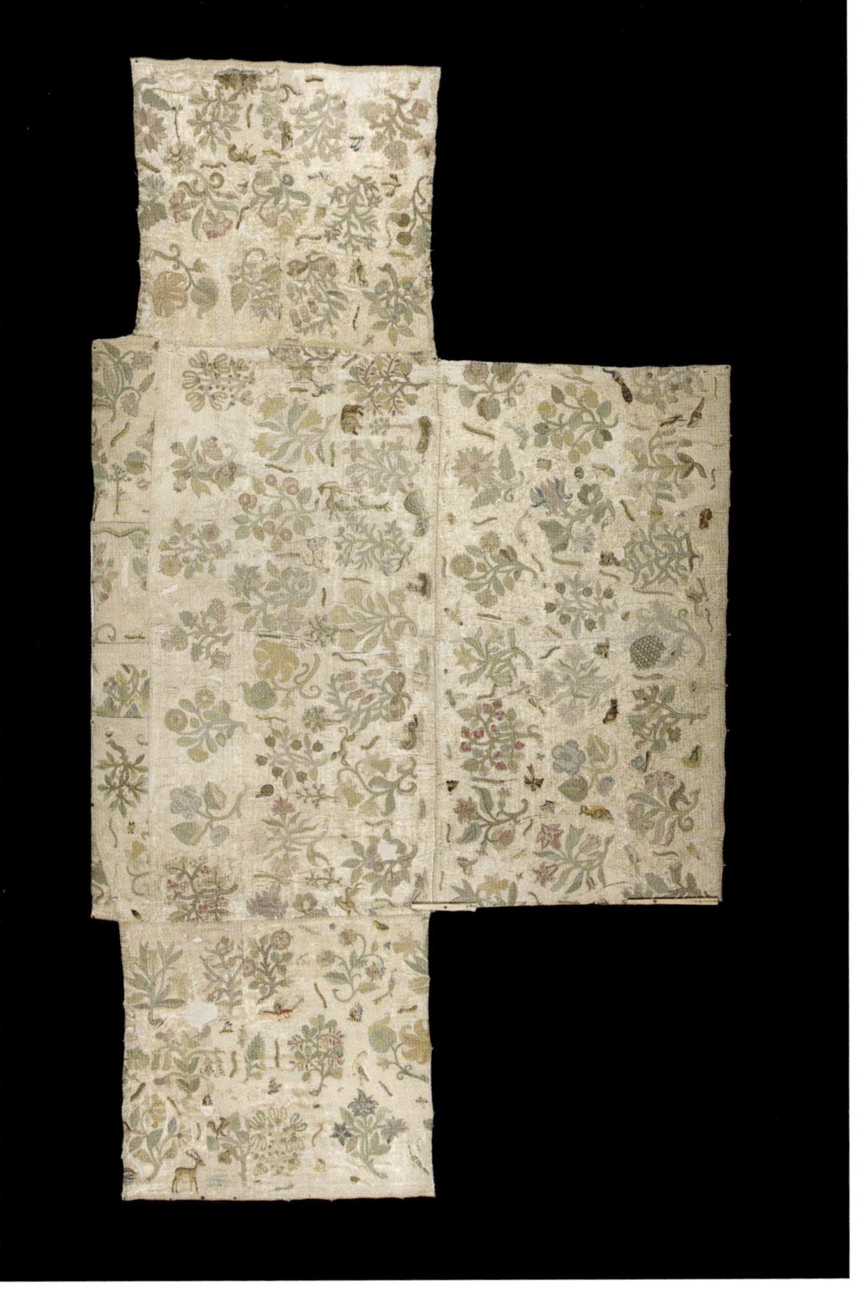

The Bacton Altar Cloth is the only surviving material from any of Elizabeth's extensive and impressive wardrobe of more than 1,900 dresses.

Blanche Parry led quickly to the possibility of it having belonged to Elizabeth I.

It was removed from Bacton to Hampton Court Palace, where a three-year conservation plan ensured its survival. As the original backing cloth was removed, it was clear that the colours of the Elizabethan embroidery had been remarkably preserved, likely aided by the subdued light of the church. The fabric was cleaned using fine cosmetic sponges to reveal the use of exotic dyes from around the world, including blue indigo from India and a red dye from Mexico.

An anonymous but supremely talented Elizabethan needlewoman embroidered this rich fabric with flowers, birds, animals and insects. Smaller motifs such as the caterpillars and the sea creatures have been worked by a second hand. To avoid damaging the delicate and expensive cloth of silver, the motifs would generally have been embroidered onto a separate piece of fabric and then sewn onto the base material, but these women have displayed the utmost skill, and their total confidence, by embroidering directly onto this expensive textile.

Multicoloured silks, such as those used in the Bacton Altar Cloth, were often combined with sequins (called spangles in Tudor times) and fine thread fabricated from precious metals such as silver or gold.

In the Hardwick Hall painting of Elizabeth, her white satin dress is minutely worked with land animals, flowers, birds and exquisite sea creatures. It is notable that portrait artists have gone to great lengths to intricately reproduce the patterns of the embroidery, illustrating the popularity and charm they held for the Elizabethans, in addition to reflecting a love of nature common to the Tudor era. For the embroiderer, inspiration came from published pattern books, herbal medicine illustrations,

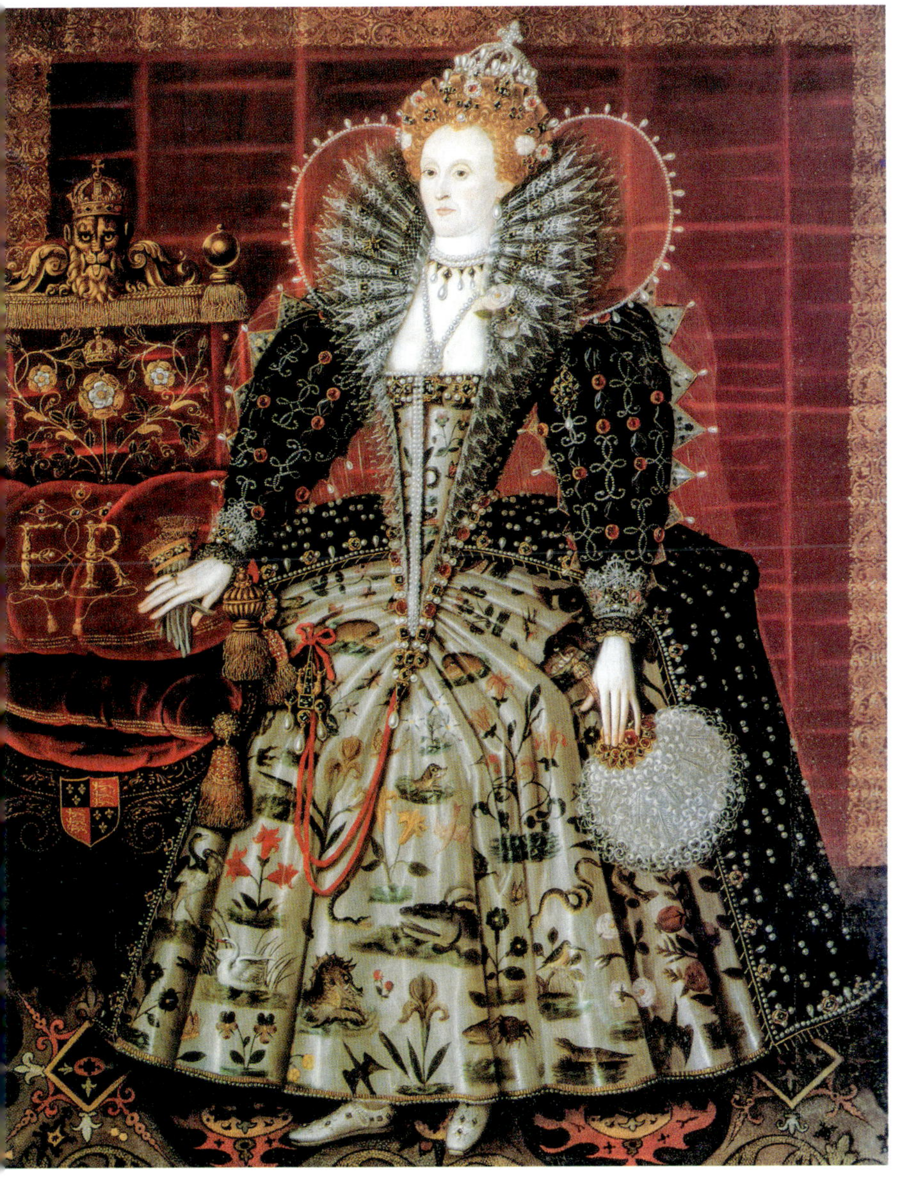

In this Hardwick Hall painting, Elizabeth's white satin dress is minutely embroidered with land animals, flowers, birds and exquisite sea creatures.

printed engravings and woodcut illustrations of animals and fish.

Needlework played an important part in the lives of Elizabethan women, but men too appear to have been skilled in the art. In the *Account of the Queen's Purse*, 1559–69, a payment of £203 15s 7d was paid to David Smith, Embroiderer, and £25 11s 11d was received by William Middleton. Large numbers of enthusiastic Tudor needlewomen and -men competed with professional workshops to produce all manner of embroidered items, from sheets, cushion covers and handkerchiefs to gloves, shoes and hawking gear.

In 1561, Elizabeth granted a charter to the Broderer's Company and by 1562 expensive, high-quality embroidered work was taken to their Hall to be inspected before being offered for sale. By 1580, there were eighty-nine Master Craftsmen of the Embroiderers Guild.

The Royal School of Needlework in England has recreated some of the motifs from the Bacton Altar Cloth to highlight the brightness of the original colours and to illustrate to future generations both the skill of Tudor needlewomen and -men and the richness and splendour of the dresses of Elizabeth I.

ELIZABETHAN SILVER

The Elizabethan period saw a rapid growth in the demand for domestic silver, due principally to the expanding population and an increasing number of middle-class families eager to buy. Skilled silversmiths responded to this new market and, from ordinary tableware to high-quality, elaborate showpieces, England was producing silver of an excellence equal to that created by continental craftsmen.

In Elizabethan homes, wooden and pewter utensils began to be displaced by silver plate and, as the century wore on, other items were fashioned in silver – sconces and mirrors being particularly eye-catching examples.

Gifts of silver were both given and received by Elizabeth on a grand scale: in 1572, she gave away almost 6,000 ounces of silver in various articles. During the first years of Elizabeth's reign, silver was highly and richly decorated in response to the influence of the Renaissance, but as her reign progressed, decoration become much plainer and evolved into simple chasing, although table salts would often be topped with an elaborate finial so that they could be seen on the table when required.

Punchbowls, snuffboxes and spoons were commonly commissioned, along with ewers and basins. William Cawdell was a London silversmith specialising in spoons and by 1599 his workshop had evolved into one of the largest spoon-making workshops in the capital. A set of spoons made by Cawdell, known as the Tichbourne spoons, was made in 1592 from silver gilt and hallmarked London. They resemble Apostle spoons, where each of the finials represents one of the twelve apostles, but in this set, Christ and St Peter are rubbing shoulders with Queen Elizabeth I.

While secular articles of silver were being produced in increasing numbers, ecclesiastical silver was being destroyed. Edward VI had ordered that all silverware employed during the Catholic Mass should be destroyed and commissioners were appointed to enter churches and remove all the plate they could find. The order was abandoned under the rule of Elizabeth's half-sister Queen Mary, but Elizabeth re-appointed the commissioners and sent them to confiscate the few remaining 'monuments of superstition'. As a consequence of this Protestant zeal, very few pieces of ecclesiastical silver made before Elizabeth's reign survive and they attain high prices today at auction.

Before the Reformation, plate made for the royal family was not always hallmarked. The Lion mark on silver was first employed around 1545 and before that, from around 1300, a leopard's head had been the standard mark for sterling silver. Precious metals are rarely used in their purest form and so a hallmark denotes the amount of pure metal contained in an item. In 1576, the gold standard was raised to 22 carats and the silver standard was confirmed as sterling.

The wonderfully named aforementioned Affabel Partridge was silver-gilt and goldsmith to Elizabeth and she patronised him more than any other. He is last mentioned in 1568, when his name is found in connection with a sale of land in Essex for £302, listed as Affabel Partridge, City of London, Goldsmith, and his wife, Dynonis. His work lives on in the collection of the Metropolitan Museum, New York, where a wine cup and cover by him are conserved. A nautilus cup, created from a shell, is in the collection of the V&A Museum, London, and a cup made by him for Sir Nicholas Bacon, Lord Keeper of the Great Seal, in the 1570s remains as testament to the skill of Elizabeth's gold- and silversmiths.

8

GOLD AND GLORY: EXPLORATION AND ARMADA

'TO SEEK NEW WORLDS, FOR GOLD, FOR PRAYSE, FOR GLORY.'

SIR WALTER RALEIGH

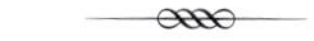

ELIZABETHAN EXPLORERS

The age of Elizabeth was an exciting time in the history of British exploration, when some of the best sailors were able to triumph with strong backing from the throne. The names which resonate with us today include Walter Raleigh, Francis Drake, Martin Frobisher and John Hawkins, all of whom were knighted for their exploits. These explorers were greatly prized for their ability to establish valuable trading routes. With improvements in navigation and the increasing accuracy of maps, ships no longer had to stay close to shore, but could cross oceans. Exploring the globe became a reality and with it the financial incentives of trading in gems, perfumes, pigments and exotic spices. England and Spain aggressively competed in the 'New World' of America and Elizabeth sponsored privateers in return for a share of the spoils they brought home.

The 'Sea Dogs' were privateers who plundered Spanish colonial settlements and treasure ships with only a licence from their queen to distinguish them from pirates. Elizabeth had no money to rebuild her navy and so the sea dogs subsidised state power by helping to combat the Spanish fleet.

A 'letter of marque' from the Queen allowed a privately owned, armed vessel to capture enemy shipping, the spoils being divided between the shipowners, captain, crew and the Crown. Letters of marque were issued by the High Court of the Admiralty to anyone who wished to take prizes and had the price of a commission, but it appears that ships were frequently taken without a letter and without declaring war, on condition that the Admiralty received a share of the booty.

In 1572, Francis Drake, the son of a tenant farmer in Devon, obtained a privateering licence and set sail in two small ships, the 70-ton *Pasha* and the 25-ton *Swan*, for America. Drake failed to capture the town of Nombre de Dios, despite a daring attack, but instead successfully plundered a mule train carrying a vast amount of silver and gold, returning home to some renown.

Thirty years after Magellan of Portugal, Francis Drake became the second mariner to circumnavigate the globe. Magellan had been killed in the Philippines after trying and failing to convert the indigenous people to Christianity and so Drake had the distinction of being the first explorer to successfully return home. It is for this achievement that he is best remembered. In 1577, five ships commanded by Drake and manned by fewer than

200 men left England with the intention of passing around South America and through the Straits of Magellan. Elizabeth did not order an official commission for this expedition, and so Drake's mission could be considered an act of piracy. With two ships abandoned, one returned to England and another wrecked, only his flagship, the *Pelican*, passed into the Pacific and along the coastline of South America. Along the way she seized provisions, valuable silver, pearls and Spanish gold coins.

In March 1579, Drake captured the Spanish treasure ship the *Nuestra Signora de la Concepcion*, taking 80 pounds of gold and 26 tons of silver, likely making him the wealthiest pirate in the world. He claimed to have sailed as far as Vancouver before being driven back by cold. Anchoring off San Francisco, he took possession of the surrounding land in the name of Queen Elizabeth I and called it 'New Albion'. He then sailed across the Pacific to the Philippines, before crossing the Indian Ocean, rounding the Cape of Good Hope and entering the Atlantic. In September 1580, laden with spices and treasures, Drake and the *Pelican* returned to Plymouth harbour having sailed around 36,000 miles.

The ship's name was changed to the *Golden Hind* and the Queen boarded it at Deptford to knight the now affluent and very famous Sir Francis Drake. The National Portrait Gallery displays a painting of Drake in fine clothing, with his motto, 'Great things from small beginnings', perfectly reflecting his rise in station.

Drake's humble origins, followed by his rise to wealth and celebrity, caused resentment among some English contemporaries. In a letter to King Philip II of Spain, a Spanish nobleman wrote, 'The people of quality dislike him for having risen so high from such a lowly family, the rest say he is the main cause of wars.' Within Spain and her empire, he was viewed as a hated pirate and heretic, known as '*El Draque*', the dragon. But, for generations of Englishmen, Drake was a national hero and the Victorians saw him and his fellow Sea Dogs as empire builders, in search of new worlds on their voyages of discovery.

SIR WALTER RALEIGH

Unknown English artist, 1588, oil on panel, National Portrait Gallery, London

Walter Raleigh was born in Devon around 1552 to a firmly Protestant family of landowners and rose to fame as a soldier, poet, explorer and Renaissance courtier. He was responsible for the first ever English colonies in the New World and holds an affectionate place in American history. It is claimed that he spoke with a soft Devonshire accent all his life and his reputation as a swashbuckling risk-taker appears to have been justified.

He left for France in 1569 and witnessed the Battle of Moncontour, near Poitiers, where Protestant Huguenots, under the command of Admiral Gaspard de Coligny, were crushed by the Catholic troops of Henri, Duke of Anjou. Returning to England, Raleigh registered as an undergraduate at Oriel College, Oxford, but left without a degree and finished his education in London.

In 1579, he went to Ireland, leading a party at the Siege of Smerwick during the suppression of the Desmond Rebellions. The siege lasted only three days but was followed by a massacre in which Raleigh led a particularly bloody attack. It saw the beheading of hundreds of Spanish and Italian soldiers, for which Raleigh received land that made him one of the major landowners in Munster.

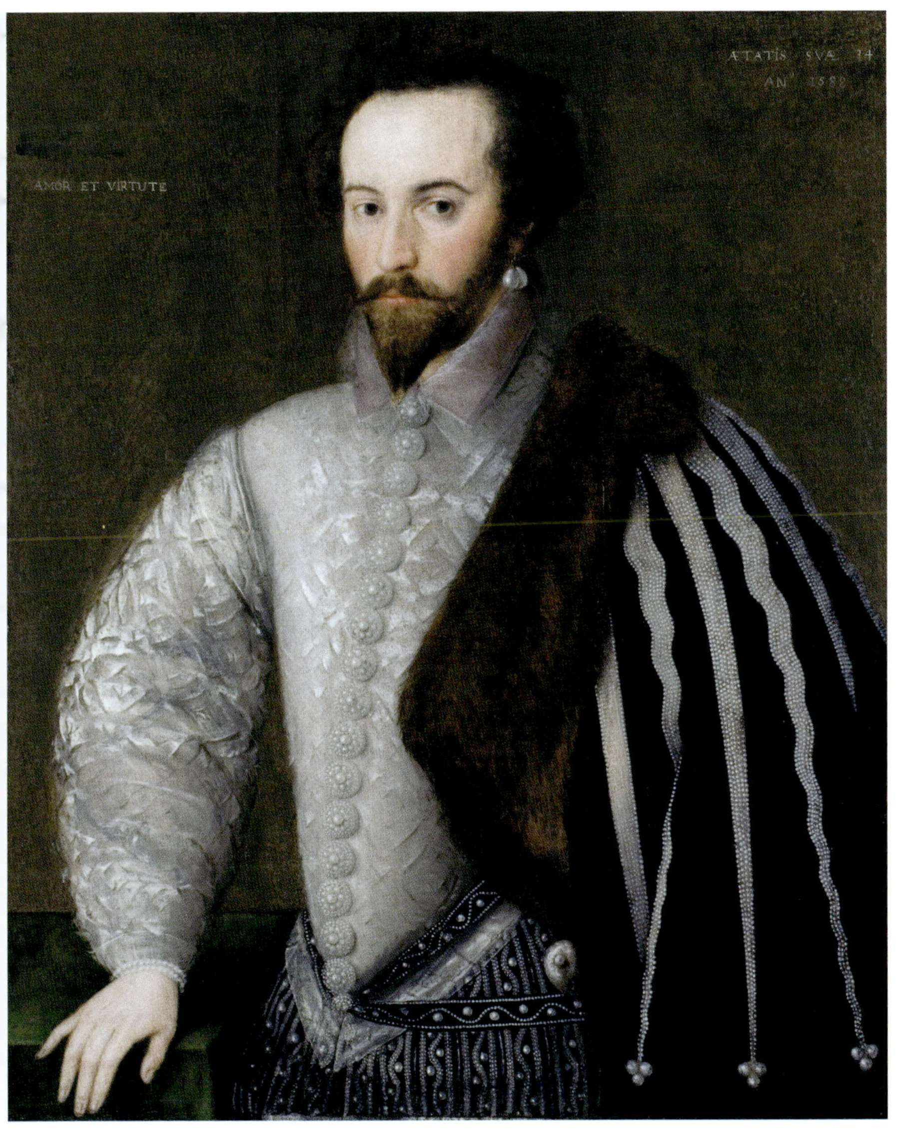

Sir Walter Raleigh rose to fame as a soldier, poet, explorer and Renaissance courtier, responsible for the first ever English colonies in the 'New World'.

It was in Munster that he met Edmund Spenser, later the author of *The Faerie Queene*, and together they travelled to Elizabeth's court in London, where Raleigh had excellent connections.

His mother, Katherine Champernowne, was the niece of Kat Ashley, who had been governess to Elizabeth. His elder brother, Carew, was a naval commander and politician, his cousin was the sailor and privateer Sir Richard Grenville and his half-brother was the adventurer and explorer Sir Humphrey Gilbert.

Tall, dark and handsome, Raleigh also knew how to participate in the 'courtly game' of gallantry. The sixteenth-century historian Thomas Fuller recorded a tale of Raleigh sacrificing his fine cloak so that the Queen might walk across a puddle. He soon became a favourite, showering her with romantic poems praising her beauty, while Elizabeth rewarded him with wealth and positions. In 1583, he was granted Durham Palace in the Strand, London, and a monopoly for wine, which brought an income of over £700 per annum. By 1586, he had been knighted and awarded lands previously belonging to the executed Anthony Babington, who had conspired with Mary, Queen of Scots, to assassinate Elizabeth.

There are few contemporary portraits of Raleigh and this triumphant depiction was painted in 1588, following the English defeat of the Spanish Armada. Raleigh did not command a ship, but he was the Queen's naval advisor and, working with Sir John Hawkins, he had been able to suggest improvements to the design of English warships that contributed to the victory.

Raleigh is here portrayed at his most swaggering, dressed in the Queen's colours of black and white. His confidence is tangible and his costume dramatic. The pearls on his cloak form the rays of a 'sun in splendour' and refer to Elizabeth. They were her signature jewels and he wears them again on his wrist and in his ear. The earring pearls allude to his daring and maverick nature and it is tempting to interpret them as a metaphor for the most masculine part of the male anatomy. They symbolise, too, his wealth and closeness to Elizabeth I. This is a portrait of Walter Raleigh, but it is one in which the Queen is strongly present.

The Latin inscription on the left reads *Amor et Virtute* ('By love and virtue') and refers to appropriate, chaste love. The lettering may be a later addition because it is not clearly visible in X-rays. On the right are the words '*AETATIS SVAE 34/ANo1588*', the sitter's age and the date of the portrait. The artist is unknown, but it has been attributed to Monogrammist 'H', perhaps the portraitist Hubbard? The lettering bears comparison with those on a portrait of Sir John Shurley of Isfield, also of 1588, in the Metropolitan Museum in New York. There are similarities between the two paintings, but Raleigh's portrait was not in sufficiently good condition to properly compare the artists.

The crescent moon to the top left of the picture frame refers to Cynthia, the moon goddess. Raleigh was a true Renaissance man who wrote about thirty poems and devoted a cycle of them to Cynthia, the alias he employed for Elizabeth I. Conservation of the panel in 2013 has revealed a line of waves below the moon, referring to the Queen's nickname for Raleigh, which was 'Water', a pun on his forename that was particularly apt considering his profession. The symbol of water also links Raleigh to the defeat of the Spanish Armada and highlights the importance of Elizabethan maritime trade.

Along with the crescent moon, the message is that the moon controls the seas in the same way that Raleigh is controlled by his queen. However, although Raleigh is presenting himself as the Queen's devoted servant, he was in a precarious position. He was vulnerable because he was wholly reliant on her patronage and, probably due to his intrepid nature, he often fell out of favour. In 1592, he secretly married Bess Throckmorton, daughter of the diplomat Nicholas Throckmorton and cousin of Francis Throckmorton. Bess was one of Elizabeth's ladies-in-waiting and their marriage without her permission (which would have been refused) resulted in them both being sent to the Tower of London.

While imprisoned, Raleigh wrote of his predicament in his eleventh and last book of *Ocean to Scinthia*, 'What storms so great but Cinthias beame appeased? What rage so fierce that love could not allay?' He was later released and permitted to return to court, principally because the Queen profited considerably from his privateering. The Royal Charter that Elizabeth had awarded him in 1584 authorised him to 'explore, colonise and rule' 'any heathen and barbarous land' on condition that one fifth of all gold and silver discovered was paid to the Crown.

From the 1580s, Raleigh's ambition was to colonise land in the Americas and to release the Spanish hold. In 1585, Roanoke, land in modern North Carolina, was explored on Raleigh's initiative and he named it 'Virginia' in Elizabeth's honour. The attempt to colonise failed and a second expedition was sent in 1587 that included John Whyte, an artist and map maker, to produce records of the land and its layout.

Raleigh later led an expedition to Guiana and Venezuela in search of the legendary golden city of El Dorado, understood to be a place of great wealth ruled by a king who covered himself with gold from head to toe each morning, washing it off in a sacred lake after sunset. Raleigh believed it to be the town of Manoa, on the shores of the mythical Lake Parime in South America, but the city was never located.

He is credited with bringing the potato and tobacco to Europe, though it appears that the Spanish were already aware of both these commodities. Raleigh popularised tobacco smoking, ironically declaring it good as a cure for coughs. Although it is probably an apocryphal tale, the explorer is said to have been enjoying his tobacco pipe when a servant saw smoke rising from him and, dashing into the room, threw a bucket of water over Raleigh, believing him to have been on fire.

After Elizabeth's death, Raleigh's fortunes declined rapidly. The new king, James I, wanted good relations with Spain, for whom Raleigh had been a formidable foe. He was accused of complicity in the 'Main Plot', a conspiracy against James, and once again imprisoned in the Tower of London. It was during this sojourn, from 1603 to 1616, that he embarked on his most ambitious writing project, *The History of the World*. It was intended for the young Henry, Prince of Wales, who came to visit the imprisoned adventurer. Henry delighted in tales of Elizabethan exploration and said, 'Only my father would cage such a bird.'

In 1618, Raleigh – the last of Elizabeth's Sea Dogs – was finally executed outside the Palace of Westminster and his body was buried at nearby St Margaret's Church, where it resides to this day. His head was embalmed and given to his wife. It was said she kept it in a velvet bag until she died, when it was reunited with his body in the same tomb. At his death, he was 64 and had lived well beyond his contemporaries. In the humorous history book *1066 and All That*, the authors suggest he was 'executed for being left over from a previous reign'.

Changes were made to the composition of this picture during the painting process. Raleigh's right hand was initially placed on his hip, but it was altered to rest on the table. The hand was painted before the sleeve and a space was left on the tablecloth to allow for further alterations. After the hand had been painted, the fingers were lengthened. Under-drawing marks the hand's position and the line of buttons on the doublet. The face, hair and beard, along with the magnificent pearl earrings, were the first elements to be defined by the artist and the moon and the sea the last to be added.

The work has been painted using azurite and smalt pigments, which give the whole portrait a cool tone. Looking closely at the pearls, it can be noticed that the artist has applied a yellow pigment to each individual pearl to imitate a shine.

Raleigh's collar would have been a quite highly coloured purple. It was first underpainted using smalt, a vivid blue pigment, before being overpainted with red lake. The red and the blue together would have resulted in a purple collar that would have enriched the appearance of the picture. Unfortunately, the smalt has discoloured and the red lake is now faded, but careful observation can pick out its still-pinkish tinge.

The background of the picture may have originally been intended to be yellow. It is underpainted in a greenish grey produced from yellow and black, but then painted over with earth pigments.

As was normal for this period, it was painted on wooden panel – in this case, three vertical boards of Eastern Baltic oak. From left to right, boards one and three came from trees that were felled after 1572, while board two, in the middle, was felled after 1540.

THE ARMADA

In May 1588, the Spanish Armada was assembled and ready to set sail from Lisbon with the specific aim of deposing Elizabeth I and returning England to the Catholic faith. The man who ordered the invasion was King Philip of Spain, once the husband of Mary I and now the powerful ruler of Spain, Portugal, the Netherlands and much of America. Philip's 'Invincible Armada' was also a response to years of English attacks on Spanish treasure ships and the aid Elizabeth had sent to Dutch Protestants rebelling against Spain.

The Duke of Medina Sidonia was appointed commander, aboard the flagship of the fleet, the *San Martin.* As the tide turned, he ordered the firing of a great canon, followed by the sound of bugles that summoned Spanish ships to weigh anchor and leave for England.

Priests blessed 130 enormous galleons, carrying 30,000 men, as they made their way down the river towards the sea, where a change in the weather forced them to anchor in the mouth of the Tagus. It was to be two weeks before they could finally set sail, but once again the fleet was forced by bad weather to seek shelter, this time in Corunna. Fresh supplies were taken on board, repairs were carried out and, after a month, the Armada set sail once more for England.

On 29 July, the great ships were sighted off the Lizard, Cornwall. Elizabeth had appointed Lord Howard of Effingham as her Lord Admiral and Commander in Chief, with Francis Drake as second in command aboard the 500-ton ship, *The Revenge.* The explorers John Hawkins and Martin Frobisher also commanded English ships, but Raleigh did not play a major part in the sea battle. England's navy consisted of forty-seven ships, whose number was bolstered by others, volunteered by gentry and noblemen at their own cost.

The Queen was reluctant to make war; peace talks continued even as the ships were sailing into confrontation. Fending off such a powerful enemy, the island nation had to save itself, against enormous odds. At an anxious meeting of the English Privy Council, Lord Burghley described the Armada as 'the mightiest enemy England ever had'.

On 31 July, the Duke of Medina Sidonia hoisted the Spanish standard on the top mast of his flagship, the *San Martin*, signalling that war was declared and England's battle with the Spanish Armada had begun. Alas, the story of Drake refusing to interrupt his game of bowls (saying there would be time enough to win the game and still beat the Spanish) is almost certainly apocryphal.

The English set sail in rain so heavy that the opponents could hardly see one another and – at the mercy of the weather yet again – few shots were fired. However, at dawn the next day, the damaged Spanish ship the *Rosario* was captured by Drake and towed into Torbay harbour. This was followed by an explosion aboard the *San Salvadore*, leading to it being towed into Weymouth and its artillery confiscated by the *Golden Hind*.

There was a battle off Portland Bill and on 4 August, as the Isle of Wight came into view, the Spanish were running out of ammunition. Howard ordered the *Ark Royal* and the *Golden Lion* to be in position to prevent the Spanish entering the Solent. After hours of battle, the Armada withdrew and made for the Straits of Dover, from where they sailed to anchor off Calais. With the Armada not moving, the English recognised their advantage and, on the night of 8 August, they acted. Eight old ships were filled with flammable material and, under cover of darkness, they were set alight and sent by the wind and tide flaming towards the Spanish. These 'Hellburners', as the fire boats were known, caused panic among the enemy fleet. In their rush to escape in the pitch blackness, the Armada galleons collided with one another. The *San Lorenzo* was damaged, but no Spanish ship was set on fire.

The following day, 9 August, Elizabeth travelled to Tilbury to address her troops, assembled to repel the Spanish. She was dressed in white, wearing a silver cuirass (armour consisting of breastplate and backplate fastened together) and riding a grey gelding. The Sword of State was carried before her, along with her silver helmet on a cushion. The following words have been attributed to her: 'I know I have the body of a weak and feeble woman; but I have the heart and stomach of a king, and of a king of England too, and think foul scorn that Parma or Spain, or any prince of Europe, should dare to invade the borders of my realm.' This moment, when morale was of the utmost importance, is crucial to Elizabeth's reputation as a truly great monarch. She faced the biggest crisis of her reign with unflinching bravery and resolved to 'live and die amongst you all; to lay down for my God, and for my kingdom, and my people, my honour and my blood'. Her accomplished oratory is particularly powerful because it presents Elizabeth both as a vulnerable woman, asking her troops to defend her, and as a military leader, defiant in the face of a dangerous enemy.

The Armada was now off the Flemish coast at Gravelines and in danger of running aground. The English took advantage and, led by Drake in the *Revenge*, they attacked. Three Spanish ships were sunk, with a dozen heavily damaged. Six hundred Spaniards were killed and at least 800 wounded. After nine hours of fighting, the battle came to an end when the weather once again turned against them.

At dawn the English moved in but, lacking ammunition, were unable to attack. The Armada was also low on ammunition and they ran north, closely followed by the English, determined to prevent the Spanish landing on English soil. Howard gave orders to relinquish the chase at the Firth of Forth. The English navy had won a spectacular victory over the Spanish, who had lost two-thirds of their 30,000 crew and half of their 130 ships. The English ships returned home with the loss of less than 100 men. Perhaps not fully realising the bravery of her sailors, Elizabeth is said to have grumbled that no treasure was captured.

In 1595, Drake set sail on his final voyage, to the West Indies. He contracted dysentery and died on 28 January 1596. His corpse is said to have been attired in full armour and sealed in a lead coffin when it was buried at sea off the coast of Portobello. Although many historians over the years have searched for his body, it has never been recovered.

Between 1585 and 1603, 'little' England waged an intense maritime war with the mighty Spain. Elizabeth and her Sea Dogs of legend made England a powerful force in sea trade and maritime conflict, while the defeat of the Armada ensured that anti-Catholicism became a significant part of what it meant to be English.

England's survival in 1588 was due to Spanish errors, bad weather and the problems of a long-distance seaborne invasion. But her capabilities at sea also played a central role in fending off invasion and the victory led to a surge in national pride and recognition of the country as one of Europe's most fearsome sea powers.

Hearing of the defeat, Philip II is said to have replied, 'I sent them to fight against men, not storms.' Sir Walter Raleigh thought Philip himself was to blame: 'To invade by sea upon a perilous coast, being neither in possession of any port, nor succoured by any party, may better fit a prince presuming on his fortune than enriched with understanding.'

Memories of the Armada were revived by the threat of French invasion in the Napoleonic Wars and again, in 1940, by the attack from Hitler's Germany, known as 'The Battle of Britain'. It was a story of the plucky English underdog facing a formidable foe, and the nation's darkest hour. Elizabeth's defiant speech at Tilbury and the events of 1588 had been brought to the cinema in *Fire over England*; released in the United States in 1937, its popularity helped to drum up support for Britain.

QUEEN ELIZABETH I (THE ARMADA PORTRAIT)

Unknown artist, 1588/90, oil on panel, Greenwich Maritime Museum, London

This portrait, painted to commemorate the defeat of Philip II's Spanish Armada in 1588, shows Elizabeth in triumph. She is richly dressed and painted in an attractive light, seated in majesty. Surrounding her are items intended to send out messages of glory, victory and intimidation. Here is Elizabeth at the glorious pinnacle of her later reign. The imperial covered crown sits beside her; she is now unchallenged, as Mary, Queen of Scots, was executed the year before, at Fotheringhay Castle. Another Catholic threat to Elizabeth's throne had also been removed.

The Queen is seated upright, her arms are open and she is looking unwaveringly at the viewer. Although she was around 55 when this was painted, her complexion is as smooth and pale as in her youth. The finial of the throne behind her left shoulder is in the shape of an egg, which in her younger days would have referred to her fertility but is now possibly a reference to her eternal youth and everlasting life.

Elizabeth's body is completely concealed, almost negating her gender and hinting perhaps at the price a female monarch paid for power. The huge number of pearls she is wearing around her neck, in her hair and on her gown associate her with Cynthia, goddess of the moon, whose power extended to the control of the seas. The largest of all the pearls is a magnificent baroque example hanging from a pink bow at around the level of her genitals. It is tempting to consider that had she been her father, Henry VIII, this would have been the site of a codpiece.

The ruff frames her face like the sun's rays, with her at the centre, emanating warmth, beauty and wisdom. Her abundant silver sleeves are resplendent with gold suns which continue across the front panel of her dress.

From around 1570, ruffs made from plain linen or cotton tended to be replaced by those decorated with or made entirely of lace, of which Elizabeth here wears an exquisite example. Before the 1550s, lace in English portraits is rare. It was portraits of the Queen, like this one, that led to the growing popularity and increasing complexity of lacework. Once attached directly to the dress, by the time of this painting they were separate garments tied with tassels that could be individually laundered.

The Queen has her hand on a globe pointing towards America and, specifically, to the colony that was named after her most celebrated attribute: Virginia. This indicates that in her moment of triumph this queen has ambitions that stretch far beyond Europe, suggesting she looks to secure a global position for the English nation. Unusually, her white, long-fingered hands (of which she

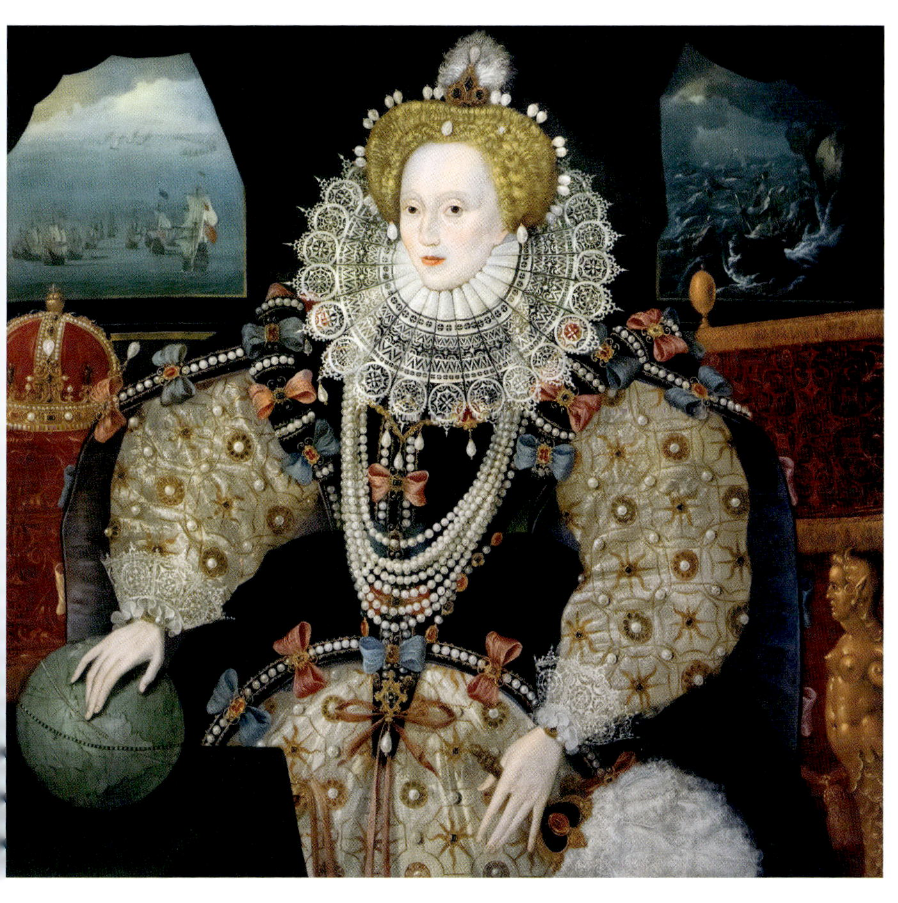

Painted to commemorate the defeat of Philip II's Spanish Armada in 1588, this portrait portrays Elizabeth in triumph, with ambitions that stretch far beyond Europe.

was so proud) are not adorned with jewellery, most likely so as not to detract from the references to the new territories lying before her.

Her dress is black and white, her preferred colours, and an expression of power and luxury. To obtain the rich black fabric, an expensive dye was required and in greater quantities than other colours to achieve the desired depth of colour. White symbolised purity and was favoured by Elizabeth for its association with virtue, but it was also considered luxurious because of the expense it took to maintain it in pristine condition. The enormous, detachable sleeves are heavily padded and embroidered with gold stars and pearls.

To the Queen's left are Spanish ships foundering in the stormy waters, on which she has turned her back. During the battle of the Armada, the fleet of Philip II of Spain was sailing to assemble around the Spanish Netherlands when the favourable wind changed to a southerly storm and they were blown north, away from their intended destination and towards the east coast of England. She looks instead to the calm seas on her right, which represent her composed leadership in taking her people away from the rough and unpredictable seas of Catholic Europe.

There is a statue-like figure to her right, reminiscent of a ship's figurehead in the form of a mermaid. Mermaids were reputed to have tempted sailors to their ruin and could refer in this instance to Elizabeth's power over the Spanish seamen. It was also a slang name for prostitutes in Elizabethan London, presumably alluding to the control they held over their clients.

This oil-on-oak-panel painting was perhaps commissioned by Sir Francis Drake; it was at one time certainly owned by him and remained in his family. Drake's cousin was Richard Drake of Devon, who had been charged with looking after senior Spanish prisoners following the Armada defeat. The Spanish vice-admiral, Don Pedro de Valdez, was held at Richard Drake's manor house in Esher. Valdez was repatriated in 1593 for a ransom of £1,500 and later became Governor of Cuba. Richard Drake named his son Francis after his famous cousin, who agreed to be the boy's godfather. Sir Francis Drake died childless and the painting was passed to his godson. It remained in the Tyrwhitt-Drake family until 2016 when it was placed on the market to secure the estate.

Following an appeal for donations by the Art Fund, 8,000 individuals contributed to its purchase. A testament, perhaps, to the affection in which it is held by the nation. In July 2016, the painting was purchased for £10.3 million. It hangs today in the Queen's House at Greenwich, which was built in the seventeenth century as part of Greenwich Palace, the birthplace of Elizabeth I. There are three known versions of this picture, all believed to have been painted around the same time. One resides in the National Portrait Gallery in London and another in the collection of the Duke of Bedford at Woburn Abbey, Bedfordshire.

The painter of this portrait is unknown, with likely suggestions being George Gower, Serjeant Painter to Elizabeth from 1581, and her limner, Nicholas Hilliard – both English artists. The three portraits are associated with different workshops but Elizabeth's face in all three versions conforms to the approved image created by Hilliard. There is a pen and ink drawing by Hilliard that was produced as part of his design for the Great Seal, in which the dress resembles the one Elizabeth is wearing in this portrait. However, as with so many Tudor portraits, we are left unable to reach a conclusion, principally because it was not customary for the sixteenth-century

English artist to leave his mark and contemporary documentation is rare.

Following its purchase for the nation in 2016, heavy layers of old varnish that dulled the colours were removed from the panel, allowing the vibrant shades beneath to shine through and offering the viewer a glimpse of the dazzling Tudor painting that Elizabeth's contemporaries would have seen.

9

DRESS, DAZZLE AND DISPLAY: MASK OF YOUTH

JOHN DOWLAND

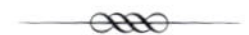

The reign of Elizabeth I was dominated by the fact that she was female. As Catherine de' Medici remarked, 'we of all Princes that be women are subject to be slandered wrongly by them that be our adversaries'.

The Queen certainly played up to stereotypes of femininity in dealing with her ministers and suitors, employing various tactics and feminine wiles: encouraging flattery, changing her mind, prevaricating and losing her temper. But she also had to be significantly different from other women. To counter criticism of her sex and unmarried status, Elizabeth and her Council fabricated a potent persona for the Queen that projected her as 'Gloriana', a female ruler who exceeds all other women.

Glorious and unchanging, she was promoted as the Virgin Queen, wedded to a country that adored her.

This image was disseminated by artists, authors and playwrights, and through the 'Cult of Gloriana' she achieved semi-mythical status within her own lifetime. The Queen mirrored the glory of the nation through her display of magnificent dresses and jewels. As previously mentioned, her ageing face was supplanted by the 'mask of youth': a smooth and ageless image created by her court artist Nicholas Hilliard. From 1596, it was a mask that all artists in England were obliged to reproduce. Even as a woman in her sixties, Gloriana was the nation's icon, always dazzling and with a face that expressed perpetual youth and immortality, in an age when beauty was synonymous with goodness.

Queen Elizabeth I (The Ditchley Portrait)

Marcus Gheeraerts the Younger, c. 1592, oil on canvas, National Portrait Gallery, London

Elizabeth is close to 60 in this portrait. The strict control that was exercised over images of the Queen may not have been fully enforced by 1592, because this unusual portrait combines the persona of Gloriana with the elderly Queen's more realistically ageing features. After 1596 her image would have been replaced by an obligatory 'mask of youth'.

She is depicted full-length, positioned on a globe, disconnected from the real world – a goddess belonging to the cosmos. Her god-like power is referenced by the armillary sphere suspended from her ear, and her feet rest on Ditchley, Oxfordshire, the home of Sir Henry Lee.

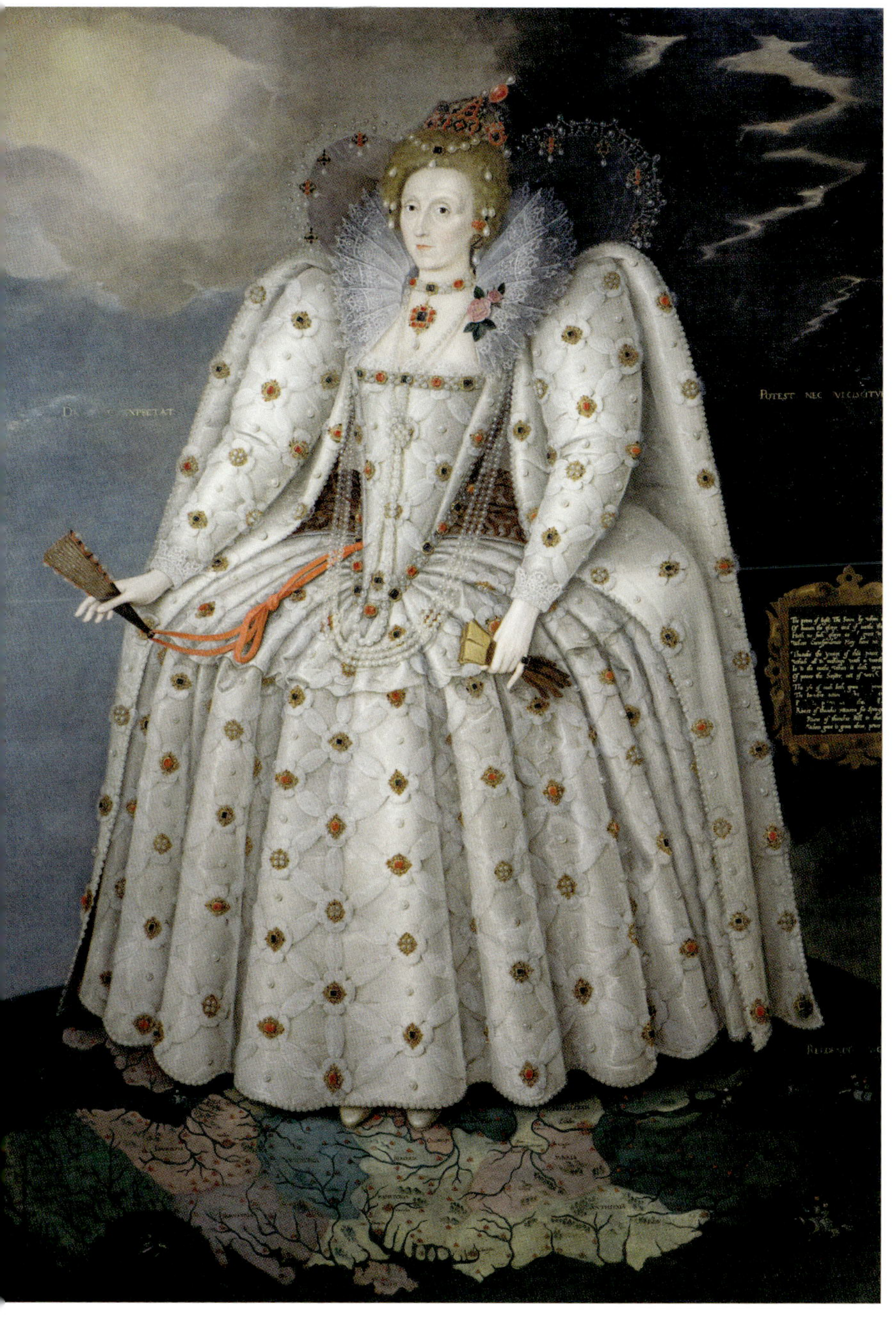

Elizabeth is depicted as a goddess belonging to the cosmos with her feet on Ditchley, Oxfordshire, the home of her former champion Sir Henry Lee.

The portrait was commissioned by Lee, Master of the Ordnance and Clerk of the Armoury at the Tower of London. He was also the first courtier, under Elizabeth, to hold the office of Queen's Champion. In a tradition dating back to the reign of William the Conqueror, the sovereign was forbidden to fight in single combat against anyone but an equal and so a Champion was appointed to battle on their behalf. Lee organised jousts for the Queen and tilted in her honour. An accomplished painting of him, by Antonis Mor, demonstrates his loyalty to his 'lady' through the celestial spheres and true-lover's knots that decorate his sleeves.

Dark clouds fall behind her and sunny skies draw near. There is a sonnet in a cartouche to the right of the picture that has been partly cut, although enough remains to learn that she is being hailed as the sun and addressed as 'the Prince of Light'.

Her white silk dress is elaborately embellished with jewels of three varied designs: gold set with an oval ruby, gold with four pearls and gold decorated with a square diamond. To ornament the complete dress would likely have required at least 135 to 140 of these impressive gems. They are mentioned in the court inventory of 1587 and many appear to have been inherited from Henry VIII, who wears similar oval ruby jewels in his 1536 portrait by Holbein.

The depiction of the gold jewels is so thorough that it is likely the artist had access to the gown without requiring the Queen to model it. It could have been positioned on a mannequin, modelled by a living woman or draped on a dress stand to permit close scrutiny. The gems appear to have been painted after the rest of the portrait was complete.

The overall effect of the work has changed since it was painted in *c.* 1592. Elizabeth's complexion would have appeared a lot warmer than it does today and her cheeks much pinker. The vermillion and red lake pigments used to create a high flesh colour have faded, making the Queen's appearance less lively. The sky was painted using smalt, a blue potassium glass that contains cobalt. When ground into a pigment, it produces an intense, rich shade. This too has discoloured, meaning the background is no longer the vivid blue it once appeared.

The canvas has suffered major damage in the past where areas of the paint have flaked, leading to the left-hand side of the heavens being overpainted and the brilliant rays of sunlight, referred to in the poem, being obscured. Although once a crucial element of the picture, the golden beams of the sun are today only visible using infrared reflectography.

Henry Lee had displeased the Queen by taking a mistress and living with her openly in his home at Ditchley. Ann Vavasour was almost thirty years Lee's junior and a married woman. She had been a lady of the bedchamber to Elizabeth and, after giving birth to an illegitimate son by the Earl of Oxford, she was now 'living in sin' with Lee and raising their own illegitimate son, Thomas. Elizabeth's disapproval of all this can be easily imagined.

Mottoes on the painting declare that 'she gives and does not expect', 'she can but does not take revenge' and 'in giving back, she increases'. These refer to the Queen's delicate relationship with Lee and his thankfulness for her forgiveness, signalled by her visit to Ditchley and her willingness to exonerate him for being 'a stranger to a lady's thrall'. A pageant – an elaborate, colourful spectacle made up of a series of tableaux and accompanied by music – had been prepared for the royal party and this portrait was likely intended as an integral part of the entertainments that took place on 20–21 September 1592.

The spectacle involved costumed figures frolicking in the grounds of Ditchley and interacting with the Queen. Her royal passage was barred by players intent on warning her that the gardens were full of distressed men and women, sick with love. Among them, lying prostrate and paralysed by desire, was an old knight representing Sir Henry Lee, who was to be liberated from death by Elizabeth. In composing the pageant, Lee was acknowledging that he was old, he was paying homage to the power of the Queen and he was requesting her forgiveness for his love of Ann.

The Queen's pardon of Lee was complete in 1597, when she appointed him to the Knights of the Garter, the most elevated chivalric order in England. He and Ann lived together at Ditchley until he died, a wealthy man, in 1611 at the age of 78. John Aubrey, the seventeenth-century English antiquary and author of *Brief Lives*, wrote of Henry Lee, 'Here lies the good old knight Sir Harry, who loved well, but would not marry.'

This painting is attributed to Marcus Gheeraerts the Younger on the grounds of his draughtsmanship and typical handling of paint, which is similar in style to his portrait of Robert Devereux, Earl of Essex. The italic style of the lettering, particularly the form of the 'W', is recognisable in other works.

Gheeraerts's father and grandfather were both artists, working in Bruges. In 1568, his father was prosecuted for producing caricatures of the Pope and for criticising Catholicism. The sentence could have been death and so he left Bruges and brought the young Marcus to London while his mother and sister remained in Belgium.

The younger Gheeraerts was most likely trained by his father, and there were additional family influences. Following his mother's death in Bruges, his father remarried to Susannah de Critz, the sister of Elizabeth I's Serjeant Painter, John de Critz. Additionally, Marcus's half-sister Sarah joined the Gheeraertses in London after their mother's death and wedded the miniaturist Isaac Oliver. Thus, within this family were two of the most talented artists of the Elizabethan period. Marcus himself married in 1590 to his stepmother's sister Magdalen de Critz, so they were truly a family of artists.

PAINTING ON CANVAS

The Ditchley portrait is the largest known full-length portrait of Elizabeth I and the first of the Queen to be painted on canvas instead of wooden panel. Marcus Gheeraerts was one of the first artists in England to paint on canvas. It was used as an alternative to panel in sixteenth-century Europe because it was cheaper, lighter and could be produced in larger sizes. Known as *cannabis* in Latin, it was historically made from tightly woven hemp. During the Renaissance, great importance was placed on preparing the canvas using gesso. This was intended to hide the weave and to ensure that the oil paint did not touch the fabric of the canvas, as it caused it to decay.

The first canvases produced for artists in Europe came from Venice, where the woven material was a common sight in the sails of ships in the lagoon. The humid climate of the Venetian bay meant that frescoes were not stable and wooden panels absorbed the moisture and warped, so an alternative was sought. Paintings on canvas could be larger and were more portable because they could be rolled up for transportation. Spanish artists soon followed the Italians, and Northern Europe began to commonly use canvas towards the end of the sixteenth century.

However, for fine details, painting on panel still had an advantage because of its smooth surface.

DRESS

As Elizabeth's reign progressed, her clothing became ever more complex and dramatic. She wore hundreds of spangles, braiding and little jewels which sparkled and caught the light when she moved. The task of dressing her fell to the ladies of the bedchamber and it would have taken more than an hour, principally because each part of the ensemble was assembled and tied on separately. It would not have been possible for the Queen to dress herself, even if she wished to, for each layer of clothing had to be fastened with laces, and hundreds of pins were required to keep intricate pieces in place, layer after layer.

The first item of clothing on the Queen's body was a smock or chemise, probably sewn from soft linen. It would have been worn as an undergarment for comfort and to avoid staining the silk satin dresses with perspiration.

BODIES FROM THE EFFIGY OF ELIZABETH I

c. 1603, Westminster Abbey, London

Over the chemise a boned corset, referred to as a pair of 'bodies', flattened the bust and elongated the waist, fastening at either the front or the back. On her death in 1603, a funeral effigy of Elizabeth I was made from wood and placed on top of the coffin. The figure was remade in 1760 and a wax head was added, but the original bodies from 1603 survive and can be viewed at Westminster

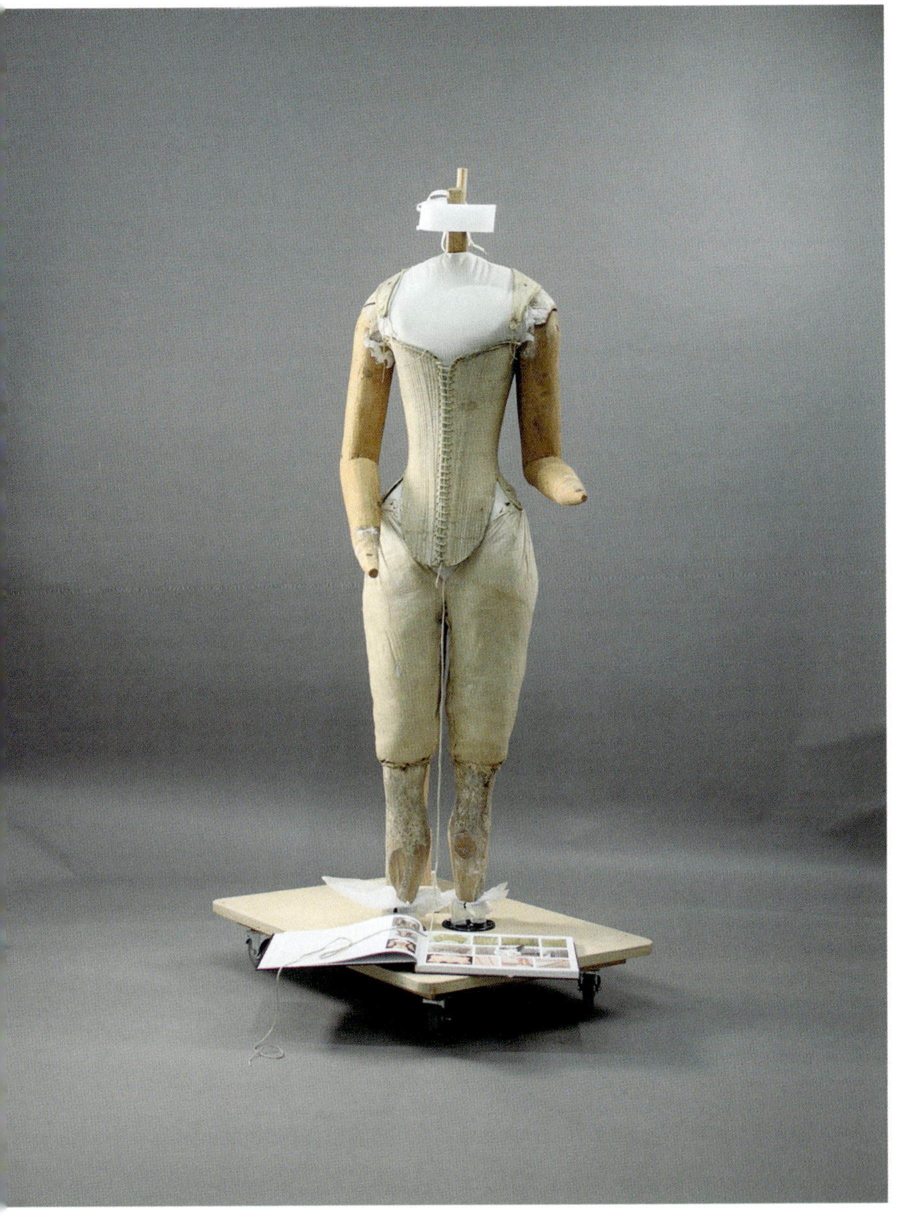

Boned corset from the effigy of Elizabeth I at Westminster Abbey. The very narrow shape is testament to Elizabeth's slender figure, even in old age.

Abbey. They are probably of the style the Queen wore at the end of her life – front laced and boned with whalebone in strips of around a quarter inch wide. Their very narrow size is testament to Elizabeth's slender figure, even in old age.

It has been thought that women did not wear knickers or drawers until the end of the eighteenth century, but the accounts of the Great Wardrobe (1558 to 1603) note that John Colte, who made the wooden effigy of the Queen, was paid £10 to provide 'the image representing her majestie … with one paire of straite bodies (corsets) and a paire of drawers'. The Englishman Fynes Moryson, who spent most of the 1590s travelling Europe and writing about his adventures, noted that 'many Italian ladies wear silk or linen breeches under their gowns', and Marie de' Medici is believed to have had many pairs of drawers made for her. However, Elizabeth's underwear habits remain something of a mystery.

In 1559, she was presented with her first pair of silk stockings, to replace the cloth ones she usually wore, and was so impressed that she vowed never to wear anything else but silk. They were held up with ribbons that tied just below the knee. There is a pair of her silk stockings – thought to be among the first in England – at Hatfield House.

With the chemise, the corset and the stockings in place, it was time to tie on the farthingale. A padded roll was first tied around the waist and a wheel-shaped structure made from whalebone or even metal placed on top. This structure changed shape according to fashion during Elizabeth's reign, but in the Ditchley portrait she is wearing a wheel farthingale, which was popular in Europe from around 1590. The attraction of a farthingale was that it spread the fabric of the dress and displayed the expensive material to best advantage. It was fashionable for the hemline to be lower at the front and to rise shorter at the back. The same silhouette was copied by Elizabeth's ladies, but the most expensive material and elaborately jewelled decorations were intended to set the Queen apart from the rest of the court.

A tight-fitting bodice was put on next. It had a deep V-shaped opening into which a stiffened piece of fabric known as a stomacher was pinned or tied. The lengths of fabric floating from the Queen's shoulders in the Ditchley portrait are known as 'hanging sleeves' but they were worn simply as decoration, the 'true' sleeves being tied to the bodice. At the back of the Queen's gown is a brocade overskirt in a different design to the dress. A heavily gathered 'proper' skirt was tied around the waist and fell to the floor at the front.

The open-style ruff that Elizabeth wears is usually associated with unmarried women and behind it is a wired veil with lace cuffs on her wrists to match. Ruffs were made of varying kinds of linen, either Lawne, Holland or Camerick, all finely woven and expensive. They were starched, a skill at which the Dutch excelled, and were generally white. Wearing a ruff in the open air could be unpredictable, because if caught in an unexpected rainstorm they would collapse. If in doubt, the ruff could be carried in a box and tied on by your maid on arrival.

Gloves and fans were often received as diplomatic gifts and the folding fan in this portrait was a modern novelty, more unusual than the feather variety. Fans were delicate items and generally stored in leather boxes lined with taffeta. Gloves were usually sewn from the finest leather and often strongly perfumed, something the Queen appears to have disliked. The fingers of the gloves were sewn exaggeratedly long with the tips padded with fine wool to elongate the hands and show off her elegant fingers.

Elizabeth's shoes in the portrait were likely made from silk satin to match her dress and she appears to have favoured slip-on shoes with a thin sole and low heel that were referred to as 'pumps', a style that would not be unfashionable today. William and Roland Winter made footwear for the Queen until 1581 and Garret Johnson made the Queen a new pair of shoes every week until 1590, when he disappears from the records and is superseded by Peter Johnson (perhaps a son). Johnson also supplied the Queen with shoehorns to ease the pumps onto her foot. The blacksmiths Polson and Jeffrey made her shoehorns of metal, but they appear not to have been as successful as those produced from softer horn.

The Queen had a fondness for footwear and on 12 April 1577 the Royal Wardrobe noted an order for 'Spanische leather shoes of sundrye colours, one pair stitched and lined with carnacion taphata'. John Parr, the Queen's embroiderer, edged a pair of shoes made of cloth of silver and in 1572 John Wynneyard is noted as perfuming two pairs of Elizabeth's shoes. The monarch was known for her parsimony and Garret Johnson submitted an account for 'translating' a pair of velvet-lined slippers, meaning cutting out the worn pieces and remaking them.

Elizabeth chose the colour of her clothes with great care. White was a popular choice as it represented purity, black was for constancy and the two together meant chastity. Red echoed the blood of Christ, mercy and justice, while red and white symbolised Lancaster and York.

DAZZLE

As evidenced by the portraits within this book, Queen Elizabeth loved jewels. Even in her old age, she maintained her public appearance and wore a great amount of jewellery. In 1587, an inventory of 628 pieces was recorded by Blanche Parry, Chief Gentlewoman and Keeper of Her Majesty's Jewels.

Many of her treasures were received as gifts from ambassadors or courtiers and some were presented to her by suitors or even looted from the ships of her Spanish enemies. On New Year's Day 1584, for example, Sir Francis Drake presented Elizabeth with gifts he had raided from Spanish and Portuguese ships. Her favourite pieces had symbolic meanings or were novelty pieces, often in the shape of ships or animals.

Hardly any of the Queen's jewellery survives today, but a particularly poignant piece is her locket ring, now belonging to the Chequers Trust. It is set with rubies, diamonds and pearl and opens to reveal two miniature enamel portraits. One is a picture of Elizabeth when she was in her forties and the other is a tiny image of her mother, Anne Boleyn. It is believed that this remarkable ring was on the Queen's finger when she died in 1603.

Robert Dudley, Earl of Leicester, is said to have begun a custom of welcoming the Queen with a lavish jewel when she came to visit his country home and, on her departure, saying goodbye with an equally precious memento of her stay. He is also said, in 1571, to have presented her with a watch encased in a bracelet (called an 'arm watch'), perhaps the first known wristwatch in England. When he died, Robert willed the Queen a diamond and emerald pendant and a rope of 600 large pearls.

Elizabeth was extremely fond of pearls, which could be worn in strands, sewn onto clothes, set into elaborate settings or worn as decoration in the hair. One of her most spectacular pieces of jewellery was a necklace of large pearls, in six strands, which once belonged to Mary,

Queen of Scots. Elizabeth outbid Catherine de' Medici of France to obtain them and they are likely to be the pearls that can be seen in several portraits of Elizabeth, including the Armada portrait (fig. 21). Pearls had an advantage over stones because they did not need cutting and polishing before being worn.

During the sixteenth century, narwhal tusk or walrus ivory was often referred to as unicorn horn and a popular myth claimed that only a virgin could stop a charging unicorn. (This is famously the subject of the *Lady and the Unicorn* tapestries in the Musée Cluny in Paris.) Elizabeth may therefore have used jewels made from tusk or ivory to reinforce her unmarried status as the Virgin Queen.

The elaborate gold settings of rings were often as prized as the jewels contained within them and sixteenth-century gemstones were cut differently from the styles seen today. Early in Elizabeth's reign, they were commonly cabochon cut, meaning they had a smooth round top, or they were table cut, leaving a flat surface, and close examination of the Queen's portraits can confirm this. Diamonds are a particularly hard jewel to fashion and so in this case Elizabethan jewellers created a pyramid cut that came to a point. By the end of the century, a rose cut had been devised that produced more sparkle and allowed the gems to glitter.

The great number of cameos of Elizabeth in sardonyx (a variant of onyx) points to a well-developed manufacturing process, although the quality is uneven and little information is available regarding the method of their production. Cameos required hard stones such as sardonyx, carnelian, jasper and onyx, with freshwater and sea pearls also used.

Brooches fell out of favour with the Elizabethans and were replaced with pendants. These jewels were fabricated from enamelled and jewelled goldwork, often incorporating large baroque pearls. (Baroque pearls are named from the Portuguese term *barroco*, meaning imperfect, and they are recognised by their irregular and unique shape.) Elizabethan pendants principally came in the form of animals; swans and other birds were favoured, as witnessed by the *Pelican* and *Phoenix* portraits. They could be worn on a ribbon around the neck or suspended from a necklace, hung from the end of a jewelled girdle (belt), attached to a sleeve or worn as an ornament in the hair.

Portraits of Elizabeth indicate a fondness for earrings. They are either a single pearl or pendant earrings with one or three pearls hanging from a central jewel, as in the *Rainbow Portrait*. Towards the end of her reign, the earring could be threaded on a ribbon which was then fed through the hole in the ear and tied with a bow, but this is not seen in portraits of the Queen.

Carcanets were wide, richly decorated gold collars set with jewels in elaborate settings with clusters of pearls, gold beads and precious or semi-precious stones. They could be worn with additional chains and necklaces to create spectacular displays. The *Pelican* and *Phoenix* portraits show good examples of the richness of these ornamental collars.

Among all of Elizabeth's jewellery, the Three Brothers jewel is both famous and mysterious. It is depicted in the *Ermine* portrait of Elizabeth (Nicholas Hilliard, 1585) and is the jewel sculpted into the tomb of the Queen in Westminster Abbey to rest with her in eternity. It was named 'Three Brothers' after the three large rubies it incorporates. They are balas rubies (after Balas in Afghanistan where they are found) of the same size and weight. A pointed diamond known as the 'Heart of the Three Brothers' is in the centre, with four pearls set around it.

It was originally designed as a shoulder clasp for John the Fearless of the House of Burgundy and he died wearing it in 1419 at the age of 33, when he was murdered by his cousin Charles Valois. It passed to his grandson, Charles the Bold, who lost the jewel and died in battle against the Swiss in 1476. It was illegally sold to the magistrates of Basel, who had a watercolour drawing made of it, making it certain that it was the same jewel worn by Elizabeth I. It was put up for sale in 1504 when it was bought by Jacob Fugger, an Augsburg financier. Fifty years later, Fugger's son began to negotiate its sale to Henry VIII, but the deal was not completed until May 1551, by which time Henry had died and it was acquired by Edward VI. Two years later, it was inherited by Queen Mary and eventually became part of the crown jewels of Elizabeth I and the early Stuarts. Of its history after Charles I, little is known. One account says that Cardinal Mazarin purchased it during the English Civil War and another says that it was dismantled. Either way, after the mid-seventeenth century, it was never seen again.

The Queen knew that her jewels played an important role in her magnificence and how she was perceived by others. Another compelling reason for her love of jewels, as Sir Francis Bacon shrewdly pointed out, was that they drew attention away from her ageing appearance. Decked out in a dazzling array of jewels and fine clothes, Elizabeth could both project an image of royal power and give the viewer an impression of beauty.

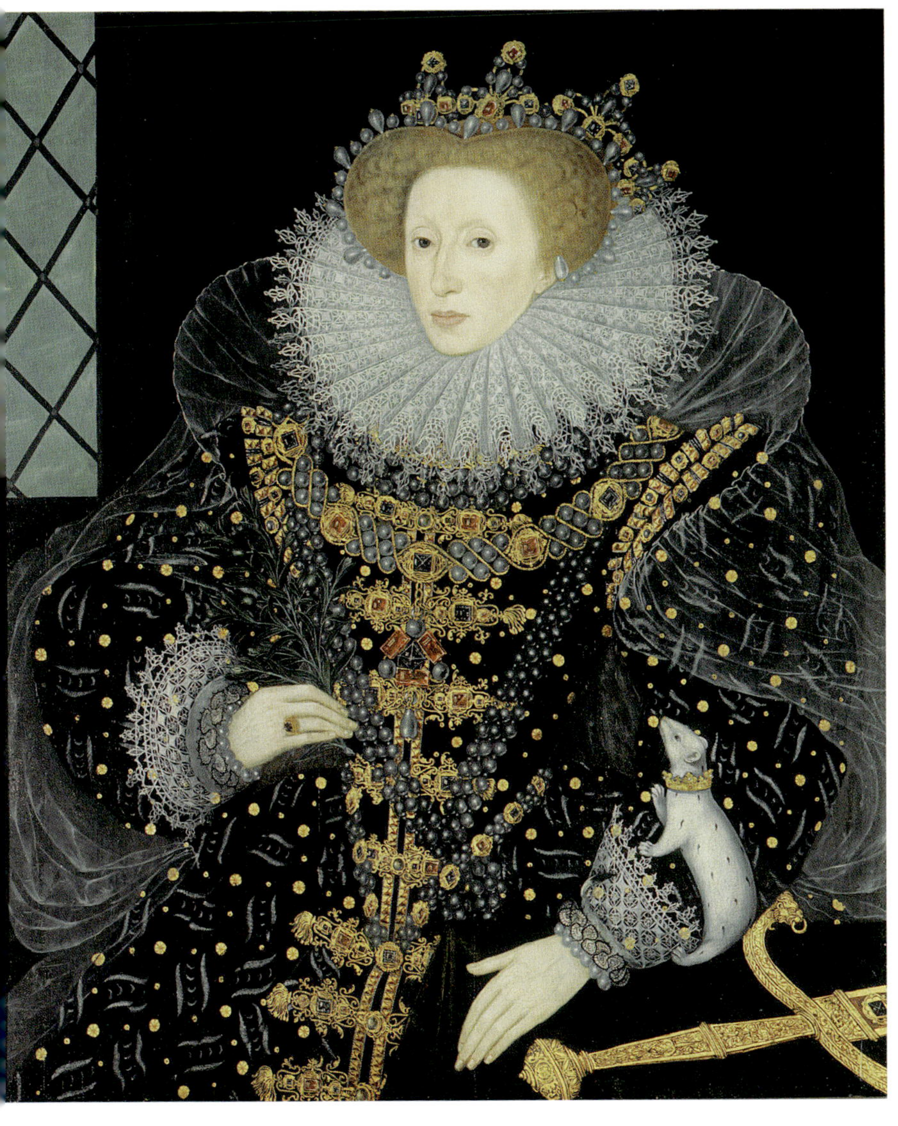

The famous and mysterious Three Brothers brooch appears (centre) in the *Ermine Portrait* and is also the jewel sculpted into Elizabeth's tomb at Westminster Abbey.

MASK OF BEAUTY

Elizabeth's appearance, with red hair, dark eyes and strong nose, is very familiar to us from her portraits, just as it was to her subjects. In her own time, her image was disseminated more than any other female figure in history, except the Virgin Mary. A profile of her, with loosely flowing hair, appeared on newly minted coins produced in the early 1560s under an ambitious programme of re-coinage. Public images were available in cheaply produced printed woodcuts and a number of portraits were made for the popular market so that ordinary citizens might view their Queen.

Although she inherited the Tudor red hair, she looked like her mother, Anne Boleyn, with a swarthy complexion, fine eyes, long, thin face and pointed chin, the same slender figure and small bosom. Like her mother, she was not a conventional beauty but she had a sense of style and a charisma that drew men to her. Beauty was associated with goodness in the sixteenth century and it was a key ingredient of Elizabeth's persona. As her own personal attractiveness faded, she would increasingly come to rely on make-up, jewels and gorgeous clothing to present an image of loveliness to her people.

It is not known exactly when the Queen started using make-up but a key event of 1562 may have prompted her decision. While at Hampton Court Palace that year, she fell ill and the deadly disease of smallpox was diagnosed by the notable physician Dr Burcot. At first, she refused to believe him and dismissed him as incompetent. However, her condition deteriorated, the tell-tale red spots began to appear and for a time she was not expected to survive. On recovery she was fortunate not to be badly disfigured, but some lesions remained from the disease. Elizabeth began to cover her scars with Venetian ceruse, a heavy white make-up made from white lead and vinegar, also known as 'Spirits of Saturn'. The ceruse could cover up any blemish but it also did great damage. As the concoction dried on the skin, it dehydrated and discoloured it, eventually leaving the complexion underneath grey and having the opposite effect to the youthful look that was intended. The Queen covered her hands, neck and face with this mixture and it could be left on her body for as long as a week. In 2020, the make-up expert Lisa Eldridge worked with a pharmacist at Keele University to recreate true Venetian ceruse, with all its toxic ingredients. The resulting mixture was creamy, opaque and pure alabaster white. Lisa discovered that, when worn in candlelight, it would have had a sheen and a beautiful ethereal glow that modern, non-toxic substitutes cannot match.

To contrast with her white complexion, Elizabeth coloured her lips and cheeks red using a paste made with red madder, a plant extract, or cochineal derived from an insect. The dye was mixed with beeswax to obtain a sticky consistency rather like lip balm. Her eyes were outlined with kohl to add definition and belladonna could be dropped into them to dilate the pupils, supposedly making them more attractive.

The facial cleanser used to remove the make-up was made from rosewater, honey, eggs and mercury, the latter making the skin feel soft but causing further poison and corrosion. The eyebrows and hairline were plucked to create a high forehead, hinting at noble birth and an intellectual personality, as seen in her *Coronation Portrait*.

The Queen's love of sugar caused tooth decay and the loss of some of her teeth. She particularly enjoyed candied violets and lavish desserts made from sugar paste, a high-status ingredient that was more expensive than honey.

Grown as a cane and imported from the East or West Indies or the Barbary coast, it was generally produced in the form of a loaf from which sugar was planed off for use. Elizabeth's ladies used wine, vinegar and honey to clean her teeth and sweeten her breath, which would have been stale from gum disease. Her sunken cheeks were sometimes padded with balls of perfumed material to plump them. In 1597, the French emissary, André Hurault, gives us a description that is far from the public image projected in official portraits: 'As for her face, it is and appears to be very aged. It is long and thin, and her teeth are very yellow and unequal … Many of them are missing so that one cannot understand her easily when she speaks quickly.'

From around the age of 30, Elizabeth took to wearing wigs fabricated in her natural shade of golden red. Smallpox had caused the loss of some of her hair and lead and mercury had thinned it. It is believed that she owned as many as eighty wigs, the style and colour of which was imitated by her court ladies. Two months before her death in 1603, a Venetian envoy describes her 'wearing hair of a colour never made by nature'.

The Queen's appearance invited compliments, flirting and flattery, and by projecting her image as Gloriana, in a cult of admiration and as the embodiment of English power, it set her apart and above her male courtiers to the end of her life.

10

FINAL YEARS: DEATH AND LEGACY

THE GOLDEN SPEECH

Henry VIII left an iconic image for posterity, as our most recognisable English king, but his daughter Elizabeth was the first great master of royal public relations. She staged a brilliant metaphorical show in which her England became an Eden and she, spectacularly dressed and bejewelled, was Gloriana, a Faerie Queen. By November 1601, she had ruled for forty-three years and was nearing the age of 70. Her health was failing and the cares of state were as pressing as ever; many loyal friends and advisors had died and she was prone to bouts of melancholy.

Against this background, she delivered a historic speech which came to stand as a symbolic end to the reign of Elizabeth I. It was heard at Whitehall Palace by Members of the House of Commons, who knelt before her expecting to be addressed on economic issues.

The purpose of a sixteenth-century Parliament was to introduce new laws by passing Acts and to raise money in the form of taxes. It was only called when the monarch wished and could be dismissed at any time. During Elizabeth's forty-five-year reign, Parliament was called just ten times and her Privy Councillors were always present to control proceedings. However, in 1601, Elizabeth decided to use the occasion for another purpose: to express her love for her country, to tell them that it would be her final Parliament and to make clear how she wished to be remembered. Most of those present had lived all their lives as Elizabethans and many wept, sensing that she was speaking to them for the last time. The oration was so powerful it became known as her 'Golden Speech' and it was printed and reprinted in the seventeenth century:

And though God hath raised me high, yet this I account the glory of my crown, that I have reigned with your loves. ... It is not my desire to live or reign longer than my life and reign shall be for your good. And though you have had, and may have, many mightier and wiser princes sitting in this seat, yet you never had, nor shall have, any that will love you better.

Elizabeth's notion of monarchy differed from her predecessors; she wished to serve her people and she claimed to have sacrificed her own personal desires for their sake. She held the love of the majority of her subjects and was rewarded with the popular epithet of 'Good Queen Bess'. The greatness and glory of the Elizabethan age are her enduring legacy.

———⊶∞⊷———

Back in 1558 the Count de Feria, envoy from Philip of Spain, had written of Elizabeth the princess, 'She is very attached to the people … and very confident that they take her part.'

As queen, she pursued a deliberate propaganda policy to ensure this popular loyalty should thrive. In prayers, ballads and speeches the English people were constantly reminded of their loving sovereign lady, who would lay down her very life for their care. The devoted relationship between queen and people was a regular theme in her oratory. She showed her compassion for the poor with charity and she went among them to touch for scrofula, a skin disease known as the 'king's evil' which it was thought could be cured by the monarch. When in procession, she might stop when a poor person tried to give her flowers or listen to petitions along the way, in well-publicised gestures. By making her people love her, Elizabeth felt safe. They would not only cheer her, with shouts of 'God save your Majesty!', but also protect her against assassination, rebellions and critics of her regime. To gain this adoration she had to show herself, parading in splendour through the streets of London or sailing on the Thames with music, gun salutes and fireworks. Her regular summer progresses allowed her to visit her nobility and gentry (at their expense) while showing herself to the common people in other parts of the country. All her life she cultivated the common touch and made a point of going amongst her people, much to the concern of her Privy Council.

Even at the age of 69, she was still appearing openly for her Accession Day celebrations in November. Although it was a risk to her personal safety, Elizabeth considered it essential that she be seen in public, as Gloriana in all her magnificence.

PROCESSION OF QUEEN ELIZABETH I TO BLACKFRIARS, LONDON, 1600/01

Robert Peake the Elder (?), Markus Gheeaerts (?), Collection of Sherbourne Castle, Dorset

Elizabeth I is depicted as a guest at the marriage of Anne, youngest daughter of John, Lord Russell, to Henry Herbert, eldest son of Edward Somerset, Earl of Worcester.

The marriage took place at St Martin's Ludgate, a medieval church situated adjacent to Lud Gate and the Roman Wall on the hill leading up to St Paul's Cathedral. The church was destroyed in the Great Fire of 1666, but the registers recording this marriage, on 16 June 1600, were saved. It was also noted by John Chamberlain, the son of an ironmonger whose inherited fortune meant he did not need to work. Between 1597 and 1626, he wrote long letters to friends abroad to inform them of events of the day. He was a moderate in matters of religion and politics and recorded social history, including the marriage depicted in this painting. He wrote to Dudley Carleton, 1st Viscount Dorchester, 'We shall have the great marriage on Monday at the Lady Russell's where it is said the Queen will vouchsafe her presence.' Elizabeth's appearance at the wedding was confirmed by him in a letter written after the wedding, dated 24 June: 'the Quene was present, being carried from the waterside in a curious chaise.'

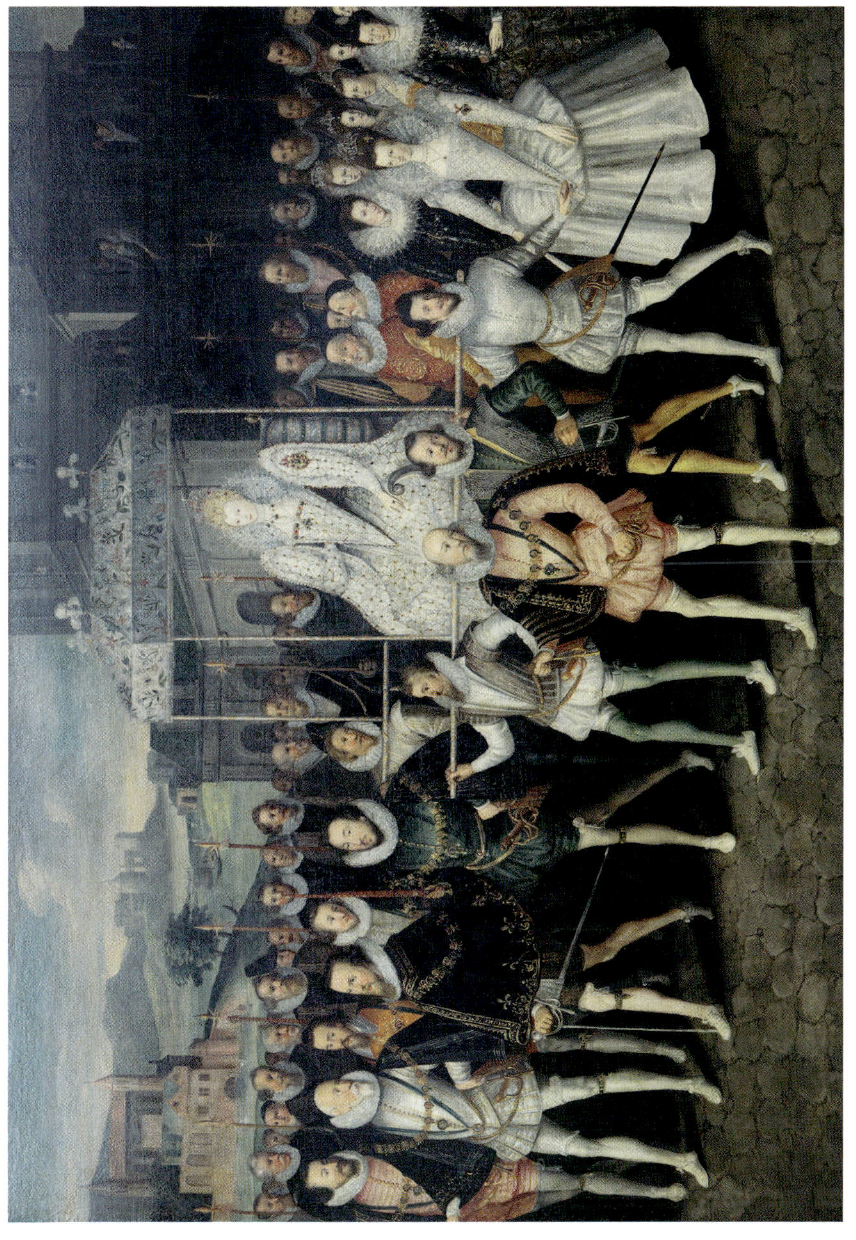

The Queen is carried by her armed guard and flanked by courtiers, while spectators watch the pageantry.

Elizabeth is wearing a white embroidered gown and is seated under an elaborate canopy sewn with flowers that has been mounted on a 'curious chaise' to raise her above the throng of people. She is almost 66, so her fresh complexion is not true to life; it is the mask of youth that Nicholas Hilliard had devised for her around ten years earlier. The open-style ruff leaves her throat and chest revealed, a fashionable style for unmarried women. The same design is worn by the bride, Anne Russell, a favourite maid of honour to the Queen and one of Elizabeth's last maids, who arrived at court in 1594. The other ladies are wearing full ruffs that probably indicate their married status. Although Anne is wearing white, a white wedding dress was not traditional at the time; generally, the bride had a new dress made or wore her best clothes in her favourite colour for the occasion.

Their route is lined with men holding halberds – weapons with blades at the end and sides. These soldiers are members of the Queen's Gentlemen Pensioners, a group of around fifty men appointed on Christmas Eve 1539 by Elizabeth's father, Henry VIII. Formed as the 'nearest guard' to follow the monarch into war, in peacetime they exhibited their sporting prowess under the direction of the Lord Chamberlain of the Household, in this case, George Carey, 2nd Lord Hunsdon. (Carey is mentioned in connection with the miniature *Elizabeth I Playing a Lute*, fig. 5.) He holds his white staff of office and walks ahead of the Queen. On ceremonial occasions, the Gentlemen Pensioners provided an escort to keep the crowd at a safe distance.

The Queen's Knights of the Garter go before her and can be recognised by their short black, embroidered Spanish cloaks and the insignia of the garter worn on their left legs. As mentioned previously, a Knight of the Garter is the most senior order of knighthood in the English honours system, to which only the monarch can grant membership. Behind the Queen are three grooms of the coach wearing white ruffs and tight-fitting black caps, their red and gold uniforms emblazoned on the front with the Tudor rose and crown.

The Earl of Worcester, father of the groom, is the bald-headed man in pink, with white stockings, at the centre of the painting. He is holding a pair of gloves that might be a gift for the bride, or perhaps for the Queen? Worcester is the most likely candidate to have commissioned this work, between 1601 and 1603, but unusually there are no arms or family insignia in the painting to confirm his patronage.

The bridegroom is Worcester's eldest son, Henry, the third bearer of the litter, wearing white and walking in front of his bride to be. He is recognised by his distinctive upturned moustache. Almost all Elizabethan men wore facial hair as evidence of masculinity; in fact, none of the gentlemen in this group is clean shaven.

Gilbert Talbot, Earl of Shrewsbury, who was appointed a Knight of the Garter in 1592, walks before the Queen. Wearing green, he holds the Sword of State, one of the most significant items of royal regalia, which is traditionally carried before the sovereign, point upwards, to represent the monarch's power to preserve right and peace.

The Elizabethan letter writer Rowland Whyte was postmaster to the court and employed by Sir Robert Sidney 'to relate to him what passed there'. He records: 'The preparation for this feast is sumptuous and great; but it is feared that the house in Blackfriars will be too little for such a company.' However, all seemed to go well: 'The gifts given that day were valued at £1,000 in plate and jewels at least, the entertainment was great and plentiful, and my Lady Russell much commended for it.'

Artistically, this work has a distinctly Elizabethan look, different in style from the art that went before and from that which would follow. Queen Elizabeth ruled over a religiously divided country and there were also vast differences between the social classes: the aristocracy, both new and old, the merchants and the manual labourers. Pageantry, chivalry and honour held a universal appeal for all levels of society and as the age progressed, this noble code that had its roots in England's medieval past became a recognisable Elizabethan cultural style.

It is a large picture in oil on cloth that is 7ft 5in. long, with figures that are 15/16″ high. It has been reduced in size, so it may have contained even more portraits, making it unique among English painting of this period. The perspective is not true, but the important aspects of the work are the detail, the portraits and the depiction of Elizabethan pageantry. It is not known where the picture originated but most likely it was produced for the Somerset family home of Raglan Castle that was destroyed by Parliamentary forces in 1646, during the Civil War.

With most art historians deciding between Robert Peake the Elder and Marcus Gheeraerts the Younger, the identity of the artist is in dispute. Peake was a native artist, born in Lincolnshire around 1551. He was the only Englishman in a close group that included Marcus Gheeraerts, John de Critz and the miniaturist Isaac Oliver, making an attribution complicated. However, Peake appears to be the most likely painter of this spectacular picture.

ELIZABETH'S ENGLAND

Elizabeth ruled a realm of extraordinary range and vitality, from the splendours of court life, the dashing adventurers, the bustling capital and the flourishing ports to the squalid poverty of town and country alike. Most of our enduring images of the Elizabethans derive from the splendour and not the squalor, but it was also a time of violence, superstition and disease.

The contemporary historian Sir Thomas Smith described the structure of the English nation in *De Republica Anglorum*, published in 1583. At its head stood the Queen, followed by four groups: gentlemen (including aristocracy), citizens, yeomen and 'the fourth sort of men which do not rule'. The latter included craftsmen, day labourers, poor husbandmen and retailers who held no political or economic power but made up the bulk of the ever-growing population. Within this structure, a tiny elite lived through a period of brilliance in exploration, literature and music. There were also increased opportunities and social mobility for the middle classes, who began to commission portraits of themselves and their wives to hang in their new houses, which now boasted the novelties of chimneys and glass windows.

But life had become increasingly hard for the vast majority who still lived and worked on the land, processing virtually everything they ate, drank and wore from their own raw materials. Only a very small proportion of people lived in towns, probably not more than one in twenty. There were regular epidemics of plague, mortality rates were high, winters were colder than today and the common people endured very poor living standards. Elizabeth's subjects were overwhelmingly youthful as most people simply did not reach old age. Life expectancy was around forty years, although very high infant mortality contributes to this low average.

The gentry increasingly converted their arable land into pasture for sheep, to produce the country's chief economic asset, English wool. But the enclosing of the land added greatly to the misery of the poor, many of whom were evicted, and beggars became a feature of Elizabethan life. The authorities tried to ban vagabonds from urban areas but this was difficult to enforce. There was lawlessness both in town and country areas, for which punishments were savage. More than 6,000 persons were executed at Tyburn alone during Elizabeth's reign and whipping or branding were common. In 1598, the poet and playwright Ben Jonson, a rival of Shakespeare, was arrested for manslaughter of a fellow actor. Because of his ability to read from the Bible in Latin, he claimed 'benefit of clergy' and was tried by a more lenient ecclesiastical court. The Biblical passage traditionally used was the third verse of Psalm 51, known as the 'neck verse'. Jonson avoided hanging, but among his punishments was the branding of his left thumb.

The nation suffered particularly badly in the 1590s from inflation, unemployment, population increase and bad harvests, leading to a loss of public morale. The average wage for an agricultural worker had risen from 4*d* to 6*d* a day but its purchasing power had fallen by 40 per cent since the beginning of the century. Disastrous harvests between 1594 and 1597 doubled the price of wheat, far more ordinary people were unable to support themselves and starvation became a real prospect for many. Elizabeth's image, as the loving mother of her people, was thus undermined, for not everyone alive in the last decade of her reign would say they lived in a golden age.

FINAL YEARS

The final years of Elizabeth's reign were blighted by these economic problems and accompanied by mounting criticism from a younger generation at court. By the 1590s Elizabeth was old enough to be the grandmother of most of her courtiers, who began to consider her out of touch. 'She imagined,' wrote Francis Bacon a few years after her death, 'that the people, who are much influenced by externals, would be diverted by the glitter of her jewels, from noticing the decay of her personal attractions.' This reflects the tone of the last decade, when her control over political and economic forces began to falter. War with Spain dragged on, with fear of a second Armada, while uncertainty over the succession loomed large.

It was also the decade in which the great names of literature entered their maturity and the English theatre reached its peak. At this point, mythologising Elizabeth as a goddess came to its height. Her painted portraits became increasingly less realistic and more like icons, while the 1596 proclamation ordered destruction of any 'unseemly' pictures showing her true age. She was dependent on her jewels, wigs and cosmetics and yet, the more her looks faded, the more her courtiers praised her beauty. In the last decade of her life, she appeared to believe her own myth, accepting the attentions of Robert Devereux, Earl of Essex, who paid court to her like a lover. Essex was the stepson of her first love, Robert Dudley, and appointed Master of the Horse on his stepfather's death – an important post, close to the Queen. She also gave him lucrative concessions, including a monopoly on imported sweet wines, which became his main source of income. Elizabeth was charmed by this handsome young man, thirty years her junior. They flirted, danced and played cards together but the ambitious Essex was not content to be merely an ornament of court. Bold, temperamental and impulsive, he wanted to win glory in the war against Spain, political success on the Privy Council and the ultimate prize of succeeding Lord Burghley as chief councillor. This long-term objective was frustrated by the very able Robert Cecil, who emerged from his father's shadow in 1596, becoming Secretary of State and taking on a growing share of government business. The younger Cecil was very small in stature and hunchbacked, due to scoliosis; Elizabeth called him her 'Pygmy'. Slight and unattractive, he lacked all the swaggering charm of Essex and political life at court became dominated by the bitter rivalry of these two very different men. They both had their own spy networks and were individually in secret correspondence with James VI, each hoping to secure power in the next regime.

Elizabeth and Essex had a tempestuous relationship; on one notorious occasion, she cuffed his ear, prompting him to half draw his sword on her. The Earl was proud and insolent, taking many liberties, which the Queen usually forgave because she loved him. She appointed him to senior commands and, although in 1596 he distinguished himself by the capture of Cádiz, his military exploits were generally unsuccessful. After Essex's desertion of his command in Ireland in 1599, he burst into the Queen's bedchamber at Nonsuch Palace to defend his actions: a shocking act of disrespect. He had also seen the grey hair and wrinkled face of the Queen without her wig and make-up. Her indulged favourite had finally overplayed his hand.

Elizabeth had Essex placed under house arrest and the following year deprived him of his monopolies. In February 1601, a combination of mounting debts and ambition led him to make a desperate, foolhardy attempt at rebellion together with other disaffected nobles who were jealous of Cecil's faction. Prior to their uprising they arranged a performance of Shakespeare's *Richard II*, about the deposition of a monarch governed by evil advisors. But few rallied to their support and the insurrection failed. Essex was tried for treason and executed on 25 February 1601, privately within the Tower of London. He was 34 years old when his head fell to the executioner's axe. For all his public love of Elizabeth, the Earl had privately mocked her as 'an old woman … no less crooked in mind than in carcass'. The betrayal of her last great favourite was both political and personal and she felt it.

ALLEGORICAL PORTRAIT OF ELIZABETH I WITH OLD FATHER TIME

Unknown English artist, c. 1610, oil on panel, private collection, Corsham Court, Wiltshire

> 'To be a king and wear a crown is a thing more glorious to them that see it than it is pleasant to them that bear it.'
>
> Elizabeth I

This posthumous Jacobean portrait shows a careworn Elizabeth in a contemplative pose, seated at a table. Two plump cherubs hover above her, their left hands carrying away the trappings of earthly power: her crown and sceptre. Above them floats a laurel wreath, a symbol of nobility, triumph and victory. But this Elizabeth is the opposite of the warrior queen who vanquished the Armada in 1588. The menacing figure of Death, the enemy she can never defeat, looks over her left shoulder, clasping an hourglass with all the sand collected at the bottom. Old Father Time has fallen asleep at her right with his sickle and a broken hourglass is overturned on the table. His work is done and death has arrived.

Now the mask of youth has fallen away and we see the Queen's face, modelled on her death mask. This is Elizabeth at her most human: an exhausted, frail old woman with deep lines under her dark Boleyn eyes and her right hand supporting her head. She has given her life and energy to the cares of the realm for so many years and the weight of the burden she has carried is apparent in her face.

Her left hand clutches the Book of Common Prayer, illustrating her religious conviction. Her thumb marks the place at which she has paused in her reading, a motif used half a century earlier when Guillaume Scrots painted her as a princess with a finger placed inside her devotional book. While the messengers of God have removed the symbols of her power, her religion remains with her, not only present but in use.

There is a glow to the figure of the Queen, reflected in the silver of her gown and soft ruff, while Time and Death are in deep shadow. Elizabeth looks deeply sad, reflecting the melancholy of her later years as death gradually robbed her of her closest advisors: Lord Burghley, Sir Francis Walsingham and her beloved Robert, Earl of Leicester, had gone and then a series of deaths among her close female friends caused her great sorrow by the end of 1602. Just as in her *Coronation Portrait* the viewer was invited to see the body politic along with the body mortal, the Queen's ailing body here may be interpreted as a tired and blighted regime. The skeleton figure of Death might

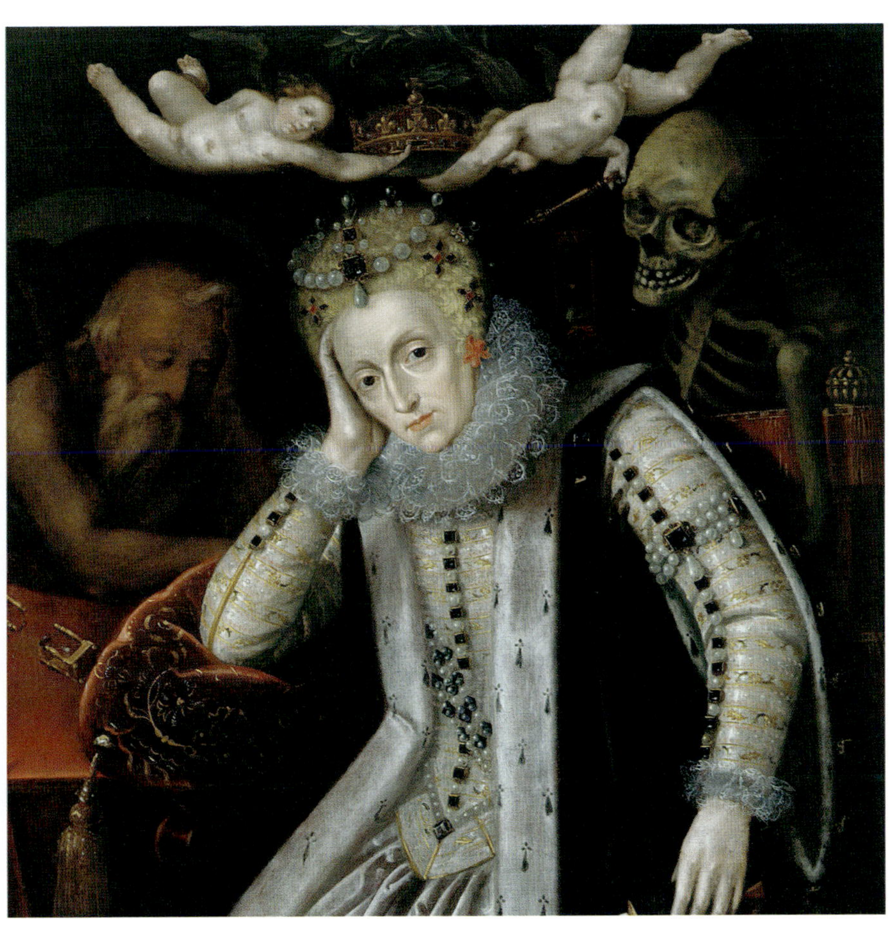

This posthumous Jacobean portrait shows a careworn Elizabeth and the melancholy of her old age. Father Time appears on the left and Death on the right.

represent the threat of starvation facing many of her subjects in the 1590s.

Conversely, while the image shows an unavoidable surrender to death and Elizabeth's awareness of her dying body, it can also be viewed as a triumph of eternity over time. The painting was probably created in the 1620s when there was a revival of interest in the Tudors and a decline in the popularity of Stuart rule. The figure Time and Queen Elizabeth are depicted as a pair in mirror image, with their heads in their hands. They have a connection, perhaps representing Time and Truth (the daughter of Time). Elizabeth will live on, in the nation's memory, as a great queen and the heroine of the true Protestant religion. In her accession portrait we were shown the body politic in preference to the body mortal. Here we are shown her aged human body, which will die, but her legacy will continue long after her death. The Accession Day celebrations continued well into the eighteenth century, with Elizabeth venerated and effigies of the Pope and the Devil being traditionally burnt on that day.

***

'She feeling some infirmities of old age and sickness retired herself at the end of January to Richmond.'
Richard Baker, *Chronicle of the Kings of England*

As Elizabeth aged, she continued with regular exercise: riding, hunting and taking brisk morning walks in her Privy Garden. She had always loved dancing and it was reported that she practised Galliards (a very energetic style of dance) every day. The Queen celebrated her 69th birthday in September 1602 and her health remained fair until the autumn, when a series of deaths among her friends plunged her into depression. She spent Christmas at Whitehall and was suffering from a cold in January when she decided to journey through bad weather to her favourite palace of Richmond, for better air. But her appetite diminished and by March she had collapsed onto cushions in her Privy Chamber, refusing to go to bed and sitting motionless for hours. Finding it impossible to take nourishment, Elizabeth grew increasingly feeble and eventually lost the power of speech. She died on 24 March 1603 between two and three in the morning, probably of bronchopneumonia. So, the Tudor dynasty ended in the palace of her grandfather Henry VII, the first Tudor monarch, who had also died at Richmond. According to the royal chaplain, Dr Henry Parry, it was a 'good death', as 'hir Majestie departed this lyfe, mildly like a lambe, easily like a ripe apple from the tree'.

Elizabeth's embalmed body was carried downriver at night to Whitehall, on a barge lit with torches. Her coffin was taken to Westminster Abbey on 23 April, watched by Londoners who lined the streets to say their farewells and mourn their dead queen. The crown passed to a foreigner – James VI, King of Scots. He was male, Protestant and the father of two healthy sons. The dazzling Tudor age was at an end.

In 1606, James commissioned a large monument for Elizabeth and her half-sister Mary, in the north aisle of Westminster's Henry VII's Chapel. The childless daughters of Henry VIII lie together, in one grave, although it is only Elizabeth's recumbent effigy that rests upon the tomb. This was made by sculptor Maximilian Colt and painted by John de Critz. The railing around the monument, decorated with the Tudor emblems of portcullis, fleurs-de-lys and roses, also bears witness to the other half of Elizabeth's inheritance: the falcon badge of her executed mother, Anne Boleyn.

LEGACY

Tudor rule ended in 1603 but it would not be long before Englishmen looked back with nostalgia to the days of 'Good Queen Bess'. Elizabeth had recognised that a monarch should rule by popular consent and the love of the people. Cecil said, 'She was the wisest woman that ever was … so perfect in the knowledge of her own realm.' Her queenship was founded on wise council and she worked in harmony with Parliament. It was a good strategy that her Stuart successors failed to follow. A contempt for Parliament and public opinion would lead to disaster in the reign of Charles I, who followed his grandmother Mary, Queen of Scots, to the block. In the 1650s Godfrey Goodman wrote of Elizabeth, 'After a few years, when we had experience of the Scottish government, the Queen did seem to revive; then was her memory much magnified.'

The Tudors were adept at handling propaganda, and none more so than Elizabeth I. So effective was the promotion of her image that, over the centuries, she has come to symbolise the national character, the beginnings of the English Church, the navy and the empire. Her England was virtually alone in late sixteenth-century Europe in averting religious war and it was headed for expansion.

Many factors contributed to Elizabeth's success, not only as a great English monarch but also as one of the greatest Britons in history. These include her intelligence and grasp of public relations, along with her ability to choose trusted advisors and to listen to them. Her father, Henry VIII, had destroyed his two most able ministers, but Elizabeth kept her best men. William Cecil, his son Robert and Francis Walsingham were among a number of shrewd, talented individuals who devoted all their energies to the Elizabethan regime. They preserved the Queen's life and her forty-five-year reign provided stability, allowing for the flourishing of English literature, led by Shakespeare, and the seafaring prowess of adventurers likes Drake and Raleigh.

The Elizabethans also witnessed the beginning of imperialism and the rise of the English language. The Queen's moderate stance shaped the Church of England and the defeat of the Spanish Armada is regarded as one of the most significant military victories in English history. Although Elizabeth followed a largely defensive foreign policy, her reign raised England's status abroad, building a new self-confidence and sense of sovereignty.

Historians have generally not been critical of Elizabeth, but it has been suggested that her habit of procrastination avoided problems rather than solving them. In foreign policy she was perhaps too cautious, giving very limited aid to foreign Protestants and failing to provide her commanders with the funds they needed. But the most serious criticism of Elizabeth is the uncertainty she caused by failing to provide for the succession or name an heir. Due to the religious divisions in the country, there was a real chance of civil war if she died suddenly.

Towards the end of her reign, economic problems certainly weakened her popularity but Elizabeth would always be remembered as a charismatic performer in the theatre of her court and a determined survivor in an age of violent religious turmoil. A long reign is an achievement in itself and a good way to ensure a lasting reputation.

Elizabeth I was a woman who achieved greatness in spite of her gender and she has been viewed as a role model for leaders of either sex. In government, she was more moderate than her father and siblings and far more lenient to transgressors. Elizabeth had been on the receiving end of royal power herself, in her sister's reign, and she didn't sign death warrants lightly.

She may have acquired royal status by accident of birth but she kept the crown through an array of personal skills which included being a great orator and possessing charisma. This queen may have lacked the prodigy of the Stuarts, but she occupies a starring role in her nation's story. By the time she died, she had reigned longer than any monarch in 200 years. An entire era of history belongs to Elizabeth.

Appendix

List of Artworks and Treasures

Introduction

Anecdotes of Painting in England by Horace Walpole,
  printed by Thomas Kirgate at Strawberry Hill, 1762.
Elizabeth I and the Three Goddesses by Hans Eworth, 1569,
  oil on panel. Royal Collection Trust, London (Hampton
  Court Palace, London) RCIN 403446.
The Marriage Feast at Bermondsey by Joris Hoefnagel, *c.*
  1569, oil on panel. Private collection, United Kingdom.

Chapter 1: Elizabeth I and the English Renaissance

Bacon cup, Affabel Partridge, 1574, silver gilt. Ashmolean
  Museum, Oxford.
Bacon cup, Affabel Partridge, 1574, silver gilt. British
  Museum, London. Museum number: 1915,0313.1.
Longleat, Warminster, Wiltshire.
Hardwick Hall, National Trust, Doe Lea, Chesterfield,
  Derbyshire.
Burghley House, Peterborough, Stamford, Lincolnshire.

Chapter 2: Family and Survival: The Early Years

The Chequers Ring. Trustees of Chequers, Aylesbury, Buckinghamshire.

Hatfield House, Great North Road, Hatfield, Hertfordshire.

Prayers or Meditations (The prayer book of Princess Elizabeth), 1545, parchment. British Library, London. Shelfmark: Royal MS 7 D X.

The Family of Henry VIII, British School, *c.* 1545, oil on canvas (support, canvas, panel). Royal Collection Trust, London (Hampton Court Palace, London). RCIN 405796.

Elizabeth I as a Princess, Guillaume Scrots, *c.* 1546, oil on panel. Royal Collection Trust, London (Windsor Castle, Berkshire). RCIN 404444.

The Tide Letter, Princess Elizabeth, Noon, 17 March 1554. National Archives, Bessant Drive, Richmond. SP 1¼/2 f.3-3v.

The Family of Henry VIII: An Allegory of the Tudor Succession, attributed to Lucas de Heere, 1572, oil on panel. The National Museum of Wales, Cardiff. Accession no: NMW A 564. On view at Sudeley Castle, Gloucestershire.

Solomon and the Queen of Sheba, Lucas de Heere, 1559, oil on canvas. St Bavo's Cathedral, Ghent, Belgium.

Chapter 3: 'God Hath Raised Me High': Accession and Religion

Coronation Portrait of Elizabeth I, unknown English artist, *c.* 1600, oil on panel. National Portrait Gallery, London. NPG 5175.

Photographs of the *Coronation Portrait* taken in 1866. Enquire archives of Victoria & Albert Museum, Cromwell Road, London.

Virginals of Elizabeth I, Giovanni Antonio Baffo?, 1570, painted cypress wood case, made in Venice, purchased in 1887 for £125. Collection of Victoria & Albert Museum, London. Accession no.: 19-1887.

Portrait of Queen Elizabeth of England playing the Lute, Nicholas Hilliard, *c.* 1576/80, vellum stuck onto card, miniature. Berkeley Castle, Gloucestershire.

The Psalter of Henry VIII, Jean Maillart 1540/41, illuminated manuscript. British Library, London. Shelfmark: Royal MS 2 AXVI.

Portrait of Elizabeth I, unknown artist, 1575, oil on panel. Reading Museum, Berkshire. Museum object number REDMG: 1980.168.1.

Chapter 4: 'One Mistress and No Master: Marriage Game

The Darnley Portrait, unknown continental artist, *c.* 1575, oil on panel. National Portrait Gallery, London, NPG 2082.

Portrait of Robert Dudley, 1st Earl of Leicester, unknown Anglo-Netherlandish artist, *c.* 1575, oil on panel. National Portrait Gallery, London. NPG 447.

The Hampden Portrait, Steven van der Meulen (or George Gower?), *c.* 1563, oil on canvas transferred to panel. Private collection, not on view.

The Sieve Portrait of Elizabeth I, Quentin Metsys II, *c.* 1583, oil on canvas. Pinacoteca Nazionale, Siena, Italy.

Chapter 5: Nicholas Hilliard: The Queen's Painter

Portrait of Henry VIII, Lucas Horenbout, 1525/6. Fitzwilliam Museum, Cambridge. PD.19-1949.

Silver gilt standing bowl, Richard Hilliard. Collection of Victoria & Albert Museum, London.

Miniature portrait of Queen Elizabeth I, Nicholas Hilliard, 1572, watercolour on vellum. National Portrait Gallery, London. NPG108.

Self-portrait at age 30, Nicholas Hilliard, miniature, 1577, watercolour on vellum. Victoria & Albert Museum, London. Accession no.: P155-1910.

Portrait of Francis Bacon, 1st Viscount St Alban, Nicholas Hilliard, 1578, watercolour on vellum. National Portrait Gallery, London. NPG 6761.

Self-portrait, Isaac Oliver, 1590, watercolour on vellum. Royal Collection Trust, London. RCIN 420034.

Portrait of Elizabeth I, Isaac Oliver, 1590/2, watercolour on
vellum. Victoria & Albert Museum, London. P.8-1940.
Miniature Portrait of Queen Elizabeth I, Nicholas Hilliard,
1595–1600, watercolour on vellum. Royal Collection
Trust, London. RCIN 421029.
The Pelican Portrait, Nicholas Hilliard, c. 1573/5, oil on
panel. Walker Art Gallery, Liverpool. Accession no: WAG
2994.
The Phoenix Portrait, Nicholas Hilliard, c. 1575, oil on
panel. Tate Britain, on view at National Portrait Gallery,
London. NPG 190.
Young Man among Roses, Nicholas Hilliard, c. 1587,
watercolour on vellum. Victoria & Albert Museum,
London. P.163-1910.
Unknown Man Clasping a Hand from a Cloud, Nicholas
Hilliard, 1588, watercolour on vellum. Victoria & Albert
Museum, London. Accession no.: P.21-1942.
Portrait of a Lady, perhaps Penelope, Lady Rich, Nicholas
Hilliard, c. 1589, watercolour on vellum. Royal Collection
Trust, London. RCIN 420020,

CHAPTER 6: SECRETS AND CODES: MARY, QUEEN OF SCOTS

The Rainbow Portrait, Isaac Oliver (?) c.1600, oil on canvas.
Hatfield House, Hertfordshire.
Portrait of Sir Francis Walsingham, attributed to John de
Critz the Elder, c. 1589, oil on panel. National Portrait
Gallery, London. NPG 1807.
Portrait of Mary, Queen of Scots, in Captivity, after Nicholas
Hilliard, inscribed 1578, oil on panel. National Portrait
Gallery, London. NPG 429
Portrait of Mary, Queen of Scots, 'en deuil blanc', François
Clouet, c. 1560/1, oil on panel. Royal Collection Trust,
London. RCIN 403429.

CHAPTER 7: ELIZABETHAN ARTS: THE GOLDEN AGE

Portrait of William Shakespeare (The Chandos Portrait), attributed to John Taylor, 1610, oil on canvas. National Portrait Gallery. London, NPG1.

The Stratford Memorial bust. Holy Trinity Church, Stratford-upon-Avon.

Portrait of Philip Sidney, unknown artist, c. 1576, oil on panel. National Portrait Gallery, London. NPG 5732.

Bacton Altar Cloth, 16th-century fabric. On loan to Historic Royal Palaces, Hampton Court Palace, London.

Portrait of Elizabeth I, attributed to Nicholas Hilliard, 1598/99, oil on canvas. Collection of the National Trust, Hardwick Hall, Derbyshire. NT 1129128.

The Tichbourne Spoons, William Cawdell, 1592, cast silver. Hampshire Cultural Trust, Winchester. Object no.: HMCMS.HCMS1975.175.

Wine cup with cover, Affabel Partridge, c. 1565, silver gilt. Metropolitan Museum, New York. Accession no.: 68.141125a,b.

Nautilus cup, Affabel Partridge, 1557/8, shell, silver gilt. Victoria & Albert Museum, London. Accession no.: M.117-1984.

CHAPTER 8: GOLD AND GLORY: EXPLORATION AND ARMADA

Portrait of Sir Walter Raleigh, unknown British Artist, 1588, oil on panel. National Portrait Gallery, London. NPG 7.

The Armada Portrait of Elizabeth I, unknown artist (formerly attributed to George Gower), c. 1590, oil on panel. Royal Museums, Greenwich. Ref: ZBA7719.

Portrait of Queen Elizabeth I, unknown English artist, c. 1588, oil on panel. National Portrait Gallery, London. NPG541.

Portrait of Queen Elizabeth I, unknown artist, c. 1588, oil on panel, Woburn Abbey, Bedfordshire.

Chapter 9: Dress, Dazzle and Display; Mask of Youth

The Ditchley Portrait, Marcus Gheeraerts the Younger, *c.* 1592, oil on canvas. National Portrait Gallery, London. NPG 2561.

Portrait of Henry VIII, Hans Holbein the Younger, *c.* 1537, oil on panel. Museo Nacional Thyssen-Bornemisza, Madrid. Inv. no.: 191 (1939.39).

Elizabeth I effigy, (remade by John Colt in 1760), 1603, wax. Westminster Abbey, London. Images can be viewed on: https://www.westminster-abbey.org/abbey-commemorations/royals/elizabeth-i.

Knitted silk stockings of Elizabeth I. Hatfield House, Great North Road, Hatfield, Hertfordshire.

Lady and the Unicorn Tapestries, 1500. Musée de Cluny, Paris. Inventory no.: 10831 -10836.

The Three Brothers Jewel depicted in the *Portrait of Elizabeth I* (The Ermine Portrait), attributed to Nicholas Hilliard, 1585. Hatfield House, Hertfordshire.

Chapter 10: Final Years: Death and Legacy

Elizabeth in procession to Blackfriars in 1600/1, Marcus Gheeraerts or Robert Peake the Elder (?), *c.* 1600/01. Collection of Colonel Wingfield-Digby, Sherbourne Castle, Dorset.

Queen Elizabeth I in Old Age, unknown British artist, *c.*1610, oil on panel. Private collection, Corsham Court, Wiltshire.

BIBLIOGRAPHY

Arnold, Janet, *Queen Elizabeth's Wardrobe Unlock'd* (London: Routledge, 1988)

Auerbach, Erna and C. Kingsley Adams, *Paintings and Sculpture at Hatfield House* (London: Constable & Co Ltd, 1971)

Bate, Jonathan, *Soul of the Age: The Life, Mind and World of William Shakespeare* (London: Penguin, 2009)

Bolland, Charlotte and Tarnya Cooper, *The Real Tudors: Kings and Queens Rediscovered* (London: National Portrait Gallery Publications, 2014)

Bolland, Charlotte, *Italian Material Culture at the Tudor Court,* (Doctor of Philosophy Thesis, University of London, August 2011)

Borman, Tracy, *Elizabeth's Women: The Hidden Story of the Virgin Queen* (London: Vintage Books, 2010)

Borman, Tracy, *The Private Lives of the Tudors* (London: Hodder & Stoughton, 2016)

Brewer, Clifford, *The Death of Kings* (London: Abson Books, 2000)

Bryson, Bill, *Shakespeare* (London: Harper Perennial, 2008)

Casey, Bart, *Anne Vavasour and Sir Henry Lee* (New York: Post Hill Press, 2019)

Castor, Helen, 'Elizabeth I: Exception to the Rule', *History Today*, Vol 60 Issue 10, October 2010

Cavendish, Richard, 'Elizabeth I's "Golden" Speech', *History Today*, Vol 51 Issue 11, November 2001

Cavendish, Richard, 'The Accession of Elizabeth I', *History Today*, Vol 58 Issue 11, November 2008

Childs, Jessie, *God's Traitors* (London: Vintage Books, 2015)

Clarke, Siobhan and Linda Collins, *The Tudors: The Crown, the Dynasty, the Golden Age* (London: Andre Deutsch, 2019)

Collins, Linda and Siobhan Clarke, *King and Collector: The Art of Henry VIII* (Cheltenham: The History Press, 2021)

Connatty, Mary, *The Armada* (London: Kingfisher Books Ltd for the National Trust, 1987)

Connolly, Annaliese and Lisa Hopkins (eds), *Goddesses and Queens: The Iconography of Elizabeth I* (Manchester: Manchester University Press, 2013)

Cook, Judith, *Roaring Boys: Playwrights and Players in Elizabethan and Jacobean England* (Cheltenham: The History Press, 2006)

Coombs, Katherine, *The Portrait Miniature in England* (London: V&A Publications, 2005)

Cooper, John, *The Queen's Agent* (London: Faber & Faber, 2011)

Cooper, Tarnya, 'Queen Elizabeth's Public Face', *History Today*, Vol 53 Issue 5, May 2003

Doran, Susan, 'Elizabeth I: Gender, Power and Politics', *History Today*, Vol 53 Issue 5, May 2003

Doran, Susan, Elizabeth: The Exhibition at the National Maritime Museum (London: Chatto & Windus, 2003)

Duncan-Jones, Katherine, *Sir Philip Sidney: Courtier Poet* (London: Yale University Press, 1991)

Dunn, Jane, *Elizabeth and Mary: Cousins, Rivals, Queens* (London: HarperCollins, 2003)

Evans, Blakemore G., *Elizabethan-Jacobean Drama: The Theatre in its Time* (New York: New Amsterdam Books, 1998)

Fraser, Antonia: *Mary, Queen of Scots* (London: Panther, 1972)

Gittings, Clare, *The National Portrait Gallery Book of Elizabeth I* (London: Scala Publishers, 2006)

Goldring, Elizabeth, *Nicholas Hilliard: Life of an Artist* (New Haven & London: Yale University Press, 2019)

Goodman, Ruth, *How to be a Tudor: A Dawn-to-Dusk Guide to Everyday Life* (London: Penguin Books, 2015)

Grant-Moss, David, 'Mutually Exclusive Goddesses: Ambivalence in the Iconography of Elizabeth I', *Interdisciplinary Literary Studies*, Vol 1, No 1, pp. 23–36, Penn State University Press, 1999

Graziani, René, 'The Rainbow Portrait of Queen Elizabeth I and its Religious Symbolism', *Journal of the Warburg & Courtauld Institutes*, Vol 35, pp. 247–295, London, 1972

Gristwood, Sarah, *Elizabeth and Leicester* (London: Bantam, 2008)

Guy, John, *My Heart is my Own: The Life of Mary Queen of Scots* (London: Harper Perennial 2004)

Haigh, Christopher, *Elizabeth I* (London: Routledge, 2001)

Hammer, Paul, 'The Last Decade of Elizabeth I', *History Today*, Vol 53 Issue 5, May 2003

Hearn, Karen, *Dynasties: Painting in Tudor and Jacobean England 1530–1630* (London: Tate Publishing, 1995)

Hearn, Karen, *Marcus Gheeraerts II: Elizabethan Artist in Focus* (London: Tate Publishing, 2002)

Hibbert, Christopher, *The Virgin Queen: A Personal History of Elizabeth I* (London: Barbara Ward & Associates, 2010)

Hilton, Lisa, *Elizabeth: Renaissance Prince* (London: Weidenfeld & Nicholson, 2016)

Hogge, Alice, *God's Secret Agents* (London: Harper Perennial, 2006)

Howard, Maurice, *The Tudor Image* (London: Tate Publishing, 1996)

Howey, Catherine L., 'Dressing a Virgin Queen: Court Women, Dress & Fashioning the Image of England's Queen Elizabeth I', *Early Modern Woman*, Vol 4, pp. 201–208, Arizona State University, 2009

King, John N., 'The Godly Woman in Elizabethan Iconography', *Renaissance Quarterly*, Vol 38, No 1, pp. 41–84, London, Spring 1985

Laslett, Peter, *The World We Have Lost* (London: Methuen & Co., 1965)

Leonhard, Karin, 'Painted Gems: The Colour Worlds of Portrait Miniature Painting in Sixteenth & Seventeenth Century Britain', *Early Science and Medicine*, Vol 20, No 4/6, Special Issue: Early Modern Colour Worlds, pp. 42 457, 2015

Lynn, Eleri, *Tudor Textiles* (New Haven & London: Yale University Press, 2020)

MacLeod, Catharine, *Elizabethan Treasures: Miniatures by Hilliard & Oliver* (London: National Portrait Gallery Publications, 2019)

Montrose, Louis A., 'Idols of the Queen: Policy, Gender and the Picturing of Elizabeth I', *Representations*, No 68, pp. 108–161, University of California Press, 1999

Mortimer, Ian, *The Time Traveller's Guide to Elizabethan England* (London: Vintage Books, 2013)

Parry, Robert Stephen, *The Virgin Queen and the Men Who Loved Her* (Independently published, 2014)

Penny, Nicholas, *Frames* (London: The National Gallery Company Ltd., 2005)

Plowden, Alison, *The Elizabethan Quartet* (Stroud: The History Press, 2002)

Pryor, Felix, *Elizabeth I: Her Life in Letters* (London: British Library Publishing, 2003)

Richards, Judith, 'Elizabeth I: Fictions and Realities', *History Review*, Issue 72, March 2012

Ridley, Jasper, *The Tudor Age* (London: Constable & Robinson Ltd, 2002)

Rowlands, Marie, 'English Catholics in the Reign of Elizabeth', *History Review*, Issue 59, December 2007

Rowse, A. L., *The Elizabethan Renaissance: The Life of the Society* (Chicago: Ivan R. Dee, 2000)

Scott, Jennifer, *The Royal Portrait: Image and Impact* (London: Royal Collection Enterprises Ltd, 2010)

Spendon Steel, H., 'The Origins and History of English Inns of Chancery', *The Virginia Law Register*, Vol 13, No 8, pp. 585–593, December 1907

Starkey, David and Susan Doran, *Elizabeth I: The Exhibition Catalogue* (London: National Maritime Museum, Chatto & Windus, 2003)

Starkey, David, *Lost Faces: Identity and Discovery in Tudor Royal Portraiture* (London: Philip Mould, 2007)

Starkey, David, *The Woman, the Queen and her Empire* (London: Random House, 2003)

Strong, Roy, *Gloriana* (London: Pimlico, 2003)

Strong, Roy, *The Cult of Elizabeth: Elizabethan Portraiture and Pageantry* (London: Thames & Hudson, 1987)

Strong, Roy, *The Elizabethan Image: An Introduction to English Portraiture, 1558–1603* (New Haven & London: Yale University Press, 2019)

Town, Edwin, 'A Biographical Dictionary of London Painters 1547–1625', *The Walpole Society*, Vol 76, London, 2014

Warnicke, Retha, 'Elizabeth I: Gender, Religion and Politics', *History Review*, Issue 58, September 2007

Weir, Alison, *Elizabeth the Queen* (London: Pimlico, 1999)

Whitfield-White, Paul, 'Patronage, Protestantism and Stage Propaganda in Early Elizabethan England', *The Yearbook of English Studies*, Vol 21: Politics, Patronage & Literature in England, 1558–1658, pp. 39–52, 1991

Willcock, Gladys and Alice Walker, *The Arte of English Poesie* (Cambridge: Cambridge University Press, 1936)

Youings, Joyce, *Sixteenth-Century England* (London: Penguin Books, 1984)